PRINCIPLES

OF

HINDU AND MOHAMMADAN LAW

PRINCIPLES

OF

HINDU AND MOHAMMADAN LAW

BY

SIR WILLIAM HAY MACNAGHTEN

EDITED BY THE LATE

H. H. WILSON

GYAN

Published by

GYAN

Gyan Publishing House
5, Ansari Road
Daryaganj, New Delhi-110002
Phone: 011-47034999, 9811692060
E-mail: books@gyanbooks.com

Distribution Network
gyanbooks.com
India, USA, Canada, UK, Australia

ISBN: 978-81-212-7023-6 (PB)
First Published, 1860

2nd Impression 2024

Printed at: Gyan Press, Delhi.

PRINCIPLES OF HINDU AND MOHAMMADAN LAW
Author: WILLIAM HAY MACNAGHTEN, Editor: H. H. WILSON

PRINCIPLES

OF

HINDU AND MOHAMMADAN LAW

REPUBLISHED FROM THE

PRINCIPLES AND PRECEDENTS OF THE SAME

BY

SIR WILLIAM HAY MACNAGHTEN.

EDITED BY THE LATE

H. H. WILSON

BODEN PROFESSOR OF SANSKRIT IN THE UNIVERSITY OF OXFORD.

FOURTH EDITION

WILLIAMS AND NORGATE,

14, HENRIETTA STREET, COVENT GARDEN, LONDON·
AND
20, SOUTH FREDERICK STREET, EDINBURGH.

1868.

INTRODUCTION.

THE acquisition of territory by the East India Company necessarily brought with it the obligation of providing for the security of person and property among those who had become subject to their rule: the local governments were accordingly authorized by Royal Charter in 1661, "to judge all persons belonging to the Governor and Company of the East Indies, or that should live under them, in all causes whether civil or criminal, according to the laws of the kingdom, and to execute judgment accordingly."

Various measures were from time to time enjoined for giving effect to the statutory provisions, but apparently with indifferent success, as in 1726 the Court of Directors complained to King George the First, "that there was a great want at the several Presidencies of a proper and competent power and authority for the more speedy and effectual administering of justice in civil causes, and for the trying and punishing of capital and other criminal offences and misdemeanours." In consequence of this representation, courts were instituted at each of the settlements, presided over by a Mayor and Aldermen selected from the most respectable inhabitants, who were empowered to try, hear, and determine all civil suits; and the Governors and Councils were authorized to try all criminal offences committed at the Presidencies, or the subordinate factories, or within ten miles of the same, whether by natives or Europeans: some modifications of this arrangement were enacted in 1753, but they were not very material, and the Mayor's courts and criminal jurisdiction of the Councils continued, until they were superseded by the successive establishments of the Supreme Courts, in which the laws of the parent country were administered by Judges appointed by the Crown, exercising jurisdiction over all British born subjects, with certain limitations as to both place and person; limitations which have been more than once matters of contest, and which it is said by high authority, are still in various cases imperfectly defined, and involve occasional doubts and difficulties.*

The grant of the Diwání, or right of collecting the revenue of Bengal, Behar, and Orissa, conferred by the titular Emperor, Shah Alem, upon the East

* See First Report of the Commission appointed in 1853 to consider the reform of the judicial establishments of India: also quoted in Morley's Administration of Justice in India, p. 19. London, 1858.

India Company in 1765, involved the administration of civil justice: that of criminal law, or the Nizámat or Faujdari courts, was in the first instance intrusted to the Nawab of Bengal, exercised through a native minister, but was subsequently also assumed by the Company's servants: in fact for some time it was indispensably necessary to confide the administration of both civil and criminal law to native functionaries, as the European servants of the Company were generally ignorant alike of the law and language of the people: their superintendence of the conduct of their subordinates was also from the same causes ineffective, and the consequences were most deplorable: agreeably to official testimony, "Extortion and oppression on the part of the public officers, and fraud and evasion on that of the cultivators, were found extensively to prevail; and the course of justice was not only suspended, but every man exercised it who had the power of compelling others to submit to his decision." *

To put a stop to this state of things, the Court of Directors in 1772 resolved to assume through their own servants the entire management of the Revenue, with the legal functions dependent upon the office. Instead of supervisors only, collectors

* Letter from the President and Council of Fort William, 1770. Fifth Report, Select Committee, House of Commons, 1812.

were appointed presiding over extensive districts, who with native assistants not only conducted the realisation of the revenues, but administered the civil law themselves, and superintended the administration of criminal law, as pronounced by the Kazi or Mufti of the district, as based upon the Mohammadan Law hitherto prevailing. Supreme courts of judicature and appeal, the Sadr Diwání, and Sadr Nizámat Adálats, were also instituted, sitting in Calcutta: the Nizámat Adálat was after a time again transferred to Murshedabad under a native judge, but it was eventually brought back to Calcutta, and united with the Diwání: arrangements of a like nature were adopted at the other Presidencies.

In the following year, 1773, the important measure was determined upon of giving to the Government of Bengal the power of making as well as administering the laws: an act, known as the Regulating Act, was passed by Parliament, empowering the Governor General and Council to frame Rules and Regulations for the good government of Bengal: these Rules and Regulations were to have the force of Laws subject to the condition of being registered in the Supreme Court, previously to being carried into effect, as a security for their comprising nothing incompatible with the laws of England: it was also enjoined that they should be translated into the native languages, and printed, both text and translation: similar powers were subsequently given to the Governors and Councils of Madras and Bombay, subject to the approbation of the Governor General in Council. The Regulations of the several Presidencies form an extensive series, access to which has been facilitated by various useful collections, analyses, digests and indices; as the Digest of those from 1793 to 1806 by Sir Edward Colebrooke; an excellent analysis of the Regulations to 1810 by Mr. John W. Harington, chief judge of the Sadr; and especially by the general collection of the Regulations and Acts of the three Presidencies, brought down to the year 1853 by Mr. Richard Clarke, formerly a member of the Madras Civil Service. Useful indices to the Regulations and Acts from 1793 to 1849 have been published by Mr. Dale, Mr. Fenwick and others.

Upon the renewal of the powers under which the Government of India was left in the hands of the Company in 1833, the Governor-General in Council was invested with authority to make laws for the whole of British India, and the legislative functions of the several Presidencies ceased; the enactments have since that time been denominated *Acts;* their registration in the Supreme Court was also discontinued, but to ensure their conformity to English statute law, a professional lawyer was introduced into the supreme Council to direct the judgment of his less learned colleagues: this arrangement has been again modified, and a separate legislative council has been organised for the purpose of framing laws, subject for their enactment to the concurrence of the Governor-General and the Home Authorities.

In all these arrangements for the administration of justice in India, the principle of reserving to its native inhabitants the continuance of their own laws and usages within certain limits, has been uniformly recognized. Upon the institution of the Mayor's courts it was provided that all suits and actions between the Indian natives should be determined among themselves, unless both parties agreed to abide by the decision of the Mayor's courts. In the plan proposed by Warren Hastings, and adopted in 1772, a clause was inserted expressly reserving their own laws to the natives, and providing that "Maulavis and Pandits should attend the Courts to expound the law and assist in passing the decree." These general reservations were more precisely defined by the Regulation Statute as finally modified in 1780, when it was enacted that "in all suits regarding inheritance, succession, marriage, caste, and other religious usages or institutions, the laws of the Kuran with respect to Mohammadans, and those of the Shastras with respect to Gentoos should be invariably adhered to." The same provision accompanied the establishment of the Supreme Court of Calcutta, and the statute enacted that "in all disputes between the native inhabitants of Calcutta, their inheritance and succession to lands, rents, and goods, and all matters of contract and dealing between party and party, shall be determined in the case of Mohammadans by the laws and usages of Mohammadans, and in the case of Gentoos by the laws and usages of Gentoos:" the same clause was introduced into the statutes by which the Supreme Courts of Madras and Bombay were instituted. The Regulations of the Indian Government were guided by the same principle, and Regulation IV of 1793 prescribes "that in suits regarding succession, inheritance, marriage, and caste, and all religious usages and institutions, the Mohammadan laws with respect to Mohammadans, and the Hindu laws with regard to Hindus, shall be considered as the general rules by which the Judges are to form their decisions." This Regulation was subsequently extended to the Upper Provinces: it had been previously enacted at Madras: at Bombay, Regulation IV. of 1797 was if possible more comprehensive, securing to Hindu and Mohammadan defendants in civil suits the benefit of their own laws regarding "succession to and inheritance of landed and other property, mortgages, loans, bonds, securities, hire, wages, marriage, and caste, and every other claim to personal or real right and property so far as shall depend upon the point of law." These statutes and regulations have never been formally repealed, although of late years very important departures from them have been hazarded in regard to succession and marriages.—Both the Mohammadan and Hindu laws enumerate difference of religious faith as a bar to inheritance. In the Bengal Regulation V of 1831, which relates chiefly to modes of procedure, a clause was inserted declaring that "the rules applicable to the observance of native laws in suits between natives previously enacted were intended, and should be held, to apply to such persons only as should be *bonâ fide* professors of the Hindu and Mohammadan religions at the time of the application to the law of the case: wherefore when one of the parties shall not be either of the Mohammadan or Hindu persuasion, the laws of those religions shall not be permitted to operate to deprive such party or parties of any property to which, but for the operation of such laws, they would have been entitled"—or in other words, a convert to Christianity from Hinduism or Mohammadanism should not thereby incur the forfeiture to which the laws of those religions would subject him: a law which, however, in our eyes reasonable and just, was undoubtedly the abrogation, as far as it went, of native law, and opposed to the faith and feelings of the people, as well as to the letter and spirit of all preceding regulations and statutes: the law was afterwards more explicitly defined and extended to the whole of British India by Act XXI of 1850, which declares that, "so much of any law or usage now in force within the territories subject to the Government of the East India Company, as inflicts on any person forfeiture of rights or property, or may be held in any way to impair or affect any right of inheritance, by reason of his or her renouncing, or having been excluded from the communion of any religion (or being deprived of caste) shall cease to be enforced as law in the Courts of the East India Company, and in the Courts established by Royal Charter within the same territories."

Another important innovation took place in 1856, when an act was passed declaring that "no marriage between Hindus should be invalid, or the offspring illegitimate, on account of any previous marriage to a person since deceased;" the object being to legalize the second marriage of Hindu widows, in contradiction to the usages and opinions of the Hindus.

The laws of the Hindus and Mohammadans are the subjects of an infinitude of elaborate and voluminous original works, for the most part composed in Sanskrit and Arabic, some few of which have been translated; a summary notice of the most important and useful will be an appropriate preliminary to the Principles of those laws which are here reprinted. The particulars are mostly derived from Mr. Morley's very excellent publication on the past history and present state of the Administration of Justice in British India, from which also the preceding recapitulation of the progress of Statute and Regulation Law has been wholly taken; the original should be consulted for a more full and detailed account.*

The Dharma Sastras, or Legal Institutes of the Hindus, comprehend a somewhat wider range than that of Jurisprudence alone: as systems they treat of three topics, Achára, Vyavahára, and Práyaschitta. By the first is intended, rules for the social and religious observances of the four castes, the Brahman, Kshatriya, Vaisya, and Sudra, and with respect to the first three, who are styled Dwijas or Twiceborn, from a ceremony which typically constitutes a second birth, the obligation of passing through the four Asramas, or orders, of student,

* The Administration of Justice in British India, its past history and present state, comprising an account of the Laws peculiar to India; by William H. Morley, Barrister at Law, etc. London. 8vo. 1858. See also Ellis on the Law Books of the Hindus, Transactions of the Literary Society of Madras, and Harington on those of the Mohammadans, Asiatic Researches, vol. x.

householder, anchorite and mendicant, an obligation little regarded in the present day. The second topic, Vyavahára, is what we mean by law, both civil and criminal. The third, Práyaschitta, or expiation, details the retribution which sin undergoes both in this world and the next. It is with the second only of these topics that we have at present any concern.

The legal institutes of the Hindus are attributed to various Munis or Rishis, sages supposed to be inspired: their compositions are considered as still to exist, and have been collected and printed at Calcutta: they are very brief, and for the most part treat only of the Achára: their authenticity may be reasonably questioned, and they are of little interest or importance; the institutes ascribed to Gautama are rather more developed, but the works of real value are only two, the Institutes of Manu, and of Yajnyawalkya: the former is well known through the early translation of Sir William Jones, published in Calcutta, and afterwards in the collection of his works: it has been reprinted with the text in a separate volume in this country by Sir Graves Haughton. The text has been twice printed in Calcutta with the commentary of Kulluka Bhatta, and an edition of the text in both Nagari and Bengali letters, with Sir William Jones's translation, and a revised version in English was commenced in Calcutta, but not continued beyond five numbers. The text with a few notes has been also printed at Paris, edited by the late M. Loiseleur Deslongchamps, who subsequently published a translation of the whole.

The text of Yajnyawalkya was printed in Calcutta with the valuable commentary of Vijnáneswara, entitled the Mitákshará, from which portions have been translated by Mr. Colebrooke and Mr. Macnaghten; the text with a German translation has been published by Professor Stenzler at Berlin.

The law books of the Rishis, even of Manu and Yajnyawalkya, although they furnish the groundwork of Hindu Jurisprudence, are not regarded as practical guides, except when elaborated by their commentators, as in the case of the Mitákshará: works of preferable weight are the systems of later jurists, or separate treatises on special topics, as inheritance, adoption, and the like: these differ occasionally in their exposition of the law, and their differences class them as belonging to different schools, of which there are three in Upper India, the Bengal, Mithila, and Benares schools, and two in the South, those of Dravida and Maháráshtra: the chief authority in Bengal is Raghunandana, who flourished in the commencement of the sixteenth century, and has left a number of treatises on the Hindu laws and customs, entitled Tatwas. These

Tatwas, twenty-eight in number, treat severally of a single topic, as the Achára Tatwa, on observances, Udváha Tatwa, on marriage, Vyavahára Tatwa, on jurisprudence, Dáya Tatwa, on inheritance, and the like: upon the subject of inheritance, Bengal possesses another standard authority in the work of Jimútaváhana, one of the two great guides in this matter, translated by Mr. Colebrooke under the title of Dáya Bhága, or portion of inheritance; the other treatise is the chapter of the Mitákshará on the same subject, which is the standard for all India, except Bengal.

The Tatwas of Raghunandana were printed in the Bengali character at Serampore in 1835, and again at Calcutta in 1840.

The Mitákshará, which differs in some respects from the Bengal law, is, as observed, of much more extensive influence, and is recognized as the standard authority in most of the schools. They are not however without their own especial guides. The principal authorities of the Mithila or North Behar school are Váchespati Misra, the author of the Viváda Chintámani, and Chandeswara, of the Viváda Ratnákara, and a lady, Lakshmidharí, to whom the Viváda Chandra and other law treatises are ascribed. In the south of India the Párásara Mádhavíya, a work of which Mádhava, the celebrated minister of Vijayanagar early in the fourteenth century, is the author, is the principal authority in Karnata and Drávida; whilst the twelve Mayúkhas, or treatises, like the Tatwas, on separate heads of usage and law, written by Nílakantha about a century and a half ago, are looked upon as the standard among the Marathas.

These are the principal original works, but there are very many other compositions, either treating of the whole system or of separate topics, that bear a character of more or less weight. They are particularised with great care by Mr. Morley.

The principle of administering native laws being admitted, it became an obvious necessity to have available means of knowing what they were, and Warren Hastings, with his usual discernment and activity, lost no time in authorizing the compilation in the first instance of a digest of the laws of the Hindus, which was compiled in Sanskrit by the end of 1773. In those days European Sanskrit scholars were rare, and it was necessary to have the work rendered into Persian, from which it was translated into English by Mr. Halhed, and published in 1774, under the title of a code of Gentoo Laws. However valuable in some respects, yet, as observed by Sir W. Jones, the translation was of no authority; for although Mr. Halhed had performed his part with fidelity, yet the Persian interpreters had supplied him with only a loose and injudicious epitome of the text, in which were many important omissions. This being the case, Sir William suggested a different compilation to be undertaken, confined to the laws of contracts and of inheritance, to be prepared under his superintendence and translated by himself. The Government of India approved of his proposal, and two works of a general character, the Viváda Sárárnava and Viváda Bhangárnava, were compiled: death prevented Sir William from effecting their translation; but the latter, "the Sea of the Solution of Legal Disputes," compiled by Jagannátha Tarka Panchánana, was translated by Mr. Colebrooke, and published at first in Calcutta in 1797, and again in three octavo volumes in London in 1801. Although this digest is defective in arrangement, and leaves many disputed questions undetermined, it is a valuable collection of authorities on the subjects to which it relates, and represents in characteristic detail the argument on either side.

These then are the principal original works from which a knowledge of Hindu Law is to be obtained, but beside these we have a variety of translations and illustrations by European writers in the service of the Company. Some of these have been noticed, as Mr. Colebrooke's translation of the Digest and of the Dáyabhága, or laws of inheritance, of Jimútaváhana and of the Mitákshará. A treatise on the law of inheritance called the Dáya Krama Sangraha was published with a translation by Mr. Wynch of the Bengal Civil Service, at Calcutta, in 1818, and a translation of the Dattaka Mimánsá and Dattaka Chandriká, two standard treatises on the law of adoption, was published by Mr. Sutherland, of the same service, at Calcutta in 1821—a French translation by M. Orianne, of the Dattaka Chandriká, and a treatise on the Hindu law of succession was published at Paris in 1844.—Translations from the Chapters of the Mitákshará treating of the course of procedure, of the Rules of Evidence, and trial by ordeal, were made by Mr. Macnaghten, and published as an appendix to his father's Considerations on Hindu Law, and as a sequel to the Principles which are here reprinted: and a translation of selected portions of the same work by Dr. Roer, with notes by Mr. Montriou, Barrister of the Supreme Court, has been recently published in Calcutta and in London in 1859.

Besides these works derived from Sanskrit authorities, we have some original compositions of the highest importance. The "Considerations on the Hindu Law as it is current in Bengal" is the work of Sir Francis Macnaghten, Chief Judge of the Supreme Court of Calcutta, and is of especial value for the illustrations it affords of the course followed by that branch of the Judicature in dealing with cases of Hindu law, and of the principles laid down by the high authority of the English Bench. Another important work of this description is the "Elements of Hindu Law chiefly as relates to the administration of Justice in India," by Sir Thomas Strange, first Chief Justice of the Supreme Court at Madras. Of this publication Mr. Morley justly observes, that it leaves little to be desired as far as regards the Hindu law of the South of India, whilst the clearness of arrangement, the aptness of the illustrations and the elegance of its diction, well entitle it to a place by the side of the commentary of Blackstone. A useful Epitome of this work by Mr. Strange, the son of Sir Thomas, was published at Madras in 1756.—Of the Principles of Hindu Law by Mr. Macnaghten we shall have further occasion to speak.

The Law-books of the Mohammadans are, if possible, still more voluminous than those of the Hindus: like them also they are based upon religion: the text of the Kuran is the primary authority, and where that is insufficieut, as it mostly is, the defect is in part supplied by the Sunna or Hadís, the sayings and doings of Mohammad, as preserved by his companions and immediate followers. In fact, however, the great body of the law, like that of the Hindus, is to be found in the writings of later jurists as systems, digests, separate treatises and collections of Fatwas or judicial decisions.

The writers on Mohammadan law are divided into two principal schools conformably to the great schism that separates the followers of Islam into the two hostile sects of Sunis and Shías, the former of whom maintain the rightful succession of the three first Khalifs, and the latter who curse them as usurpers, and recognize Ali, the son-in-law of Mohammad, as his sole lawful successor. The Suni sect predominates in Arabia, Turkey, Afghanistan, and Turkestan: the Shía in Persia: in India both sects are found; generally the educated Mohammadans are Sunis, the vulgar are Shías, and that sect also prevailed in the late court of Lucknow. The Suni code of law is that which is chiefly recognized in the Company's Courts: both sects boast of a number of able and erudite writers.

The Suni authorities are divided into a variety of subordinate schools, of whom four are recognized as the principal, that of Abu Hanífa, who flourished in the latter part of the eighth century, of Abu Abd-al Málik at the end of the same century, of Mohammad bin Idrís ash-Sháfi-î, who wrote about the same date, and Ahmad ash-Shaibáni, commonly known as Ibn Hanbal, who died A.D. 855; of these schools, the authority of the second prevails throughout Africa, of the third in Egypt and Arabia and a few places in the south of India: the fourth has but a limited currency and is rarely followed out of

Arabia, but the first, the school of Abu Hanífa, especially as developed by his disciples Abu Yusaf and Mohammad, is the principal and almost exclusive source of the Suni law in India.

The Shiás in like manner admit various, four or five, schools: their differences are chiefly on religious matters, but they also differ in some points of law as noticed in the following pages in the chapter on the Imamíya laws of inheritance, that is, the law of the twelve Imams, a title given to Ali and his descendants by the Shiás.

The authorities of Mohammadan law enumerated by Mr. Morley are of five descriptions; 1. The Kuran, with the Tafsirs or commentaries: 2. the Hadís or traditions with the works on Ijma, the decisions of the companions of Mohammad, and their disciples, the Kíyás or conclusions deduced from a comparison of the Kuran, the Sunna and the Ijma, according to the exercise of private judgment: 3. General Treatises on the fundamental principles of law and Digests of general or special law, with their commentaries: 4. Separate treatises on the law of inheritance: 5. The Fatáwa, or books of decisions: a sixth class may be formed of the works of European scholars.

In all these divisions, except the last, the writings are very numerous and many of them of high authority. The principal are named and described by

Mr. Morley, but few of them are available even to Arabic students, as they exist for the most part only in manuscript. Many of the Tafsirs or commentaries on the Kuran have of late years been printed or lithographed at the Oriental presses of Calcutta, Lucknow, Cawnpore, and Delhi, but in general the lithography is ill executed and inferior to good manuscript· the books also are not to be met with in Europe, except in the library of the East India House: of the class of traditions the same may be said, but those given to the Press are still fewer in number, although the original works and their illustrations are so numerous that Haji Khālfah, the author of the great Bibliographical Dictionary edited and translated by Professor Flügel, and published by the Oriental Translation Committee, declares it would be impossible to enumerate them.—The commentaries on the Kuran, and the collections of the Hadís have little to recommend them to European students for the light they reflect on Mohammadan Jurisprudence.

The Digests, or systems of general law, are of more practical utility, but these again are rarely accessible, not having been printed, or lithographed, or translated. An early exception to the latter was the Hedaya, the most celebrated law treatise according to the doctrines of Abu Hanífa which exists in India: its celebrity induced Warren Hastings to recommend its translation, and it was accordingly rendered into English by Mr. Hamilton and printed in Calcutta in 1791. The difficulties of the original Arabic induced the natives who were consulted, to recommend its being first translated into Persian, and it is from the latter that the English version was made: this detracts from the merit of the work, but it has been of essential service to the administration of Mohammadan Law: the original Arabic was printed at Calcutta in 1824, and was again edited with its commentary, the Kifáya, in 1834, and another commentary, the Ináya, in four quarto volumes, was printed at Calcutta in 1837: several other standard works in this department have been printed in India; standard works belonging to the same school have been printed at Constantinople, as the Multaka al Abkár with its commentary the Mujma al Anhár, which has been in great part translated into French in D'Ohsson's account of the Ottoman Empire.—Important texts and translations also of standard authority of the school of Málik have been published under the patronage of the Government of France since their occupation of Algeria, especially the Précis de Jurisprudence Mussulmane selon le Rite Malikite, translated from the Mukhtasar of Khalíl Ibn Isházk by M. Perron, and published at Paris in 1848–52 in six quarto volumes: the original text was also printed in 1855 at Paris. Of the Shiá school an extensive digest was prepared under the superintendence of Sir W. Jones, by order of the Bengal Government, and a translation of it, by Captain John Baillie, was announced, in four volumes: of these only the first was published at Calcutta in 1805.

The chief authority in India on the subject of the law of Inheritance is a treatise entitled the Sirajíya with its commentary, the Sharifíyah: the text with a translation and an abstract version of the commentary by Sir W. Jones was published at Calcutta in 1792; a second edition of the text was printed at the same place in 1829: on the Shiá laws of inheritance, a Persian treatise by Said Husain was lithographed at Lucknow in 1841, and another in the same place in 1847.

The last division of the authorities for the laws of the Mohammadans are the Fatáwa, or collections of Fatwas or Decisions: these are very voluminous and exist in considerable numbers, but are little known to European students: one of the most authoritative, printed at Calcutta by the Committee of Public Instruction in 1828, in six quarto volumes, is the Fatáwa Alemgiri: a collection that was commenced in 1656 by order of Aurungzeb or Alemgir, whence its appellation—it contains a recital of numerous cases involving almost every point of the Hanafíya law, and is consequently an authority to which reference is constantly made. Its publication, which was carefully conducted, and is handsomely printed, was highly creditable to the Government of Bengal; many other collections of a similar kind exist, as the Fatáwa Kazi Khan, a work also of high authority, which was lithographed and published at Calcutta in 1835; the Fusul Imádíya, also lithographed at Calcutta in 1827; the Kariyat al Muníyat, lithographed in 1829; the Fatáwa Hamadíya, lithographed in 1825; the Fatáwa al Sirajíya, published at Calcutta in 1827. Similar collections have been printed at Constantinople.

The laws of the Mohammadans have not been so successful, at least in point of number, as those of the Hindus, in attracting the interest of English scholars, among whom, indeed, Arabic scholarship is far from frequent: few additions have been made to Sir William Jones's translation of the Sirajíya and Hamilton's of the Hedaya; the work of Captain, afterwards Colonel Baillie, ceasing with the commencement. Of late years some valuable illustrations of the Kuran and the Hadís have been published in that valuable collection, the Bibliotheca Indica, by Dr. Sprenger and Captain Lees, but they are only indirectly connected with practical law, a subject on which we have scarcely any guides. Amongst our countrymen the only recent labourer in this field is Mr. Neil Bailly, who has published an excellent treatise on the Law of Inheritance as laid down in the Sirajíya and Sharafíya, and a work on the law of Sale selected and translated from the Arabic of the Fatáwa Alemgiri: an abstract of the Mohammadan law by Col. Vans Kennedy is given in the second volume of the Journal of the Royal Asiatic Society; the Criminal Law, based upon that of the Mohammadans as modified by the Regulations, is fully treated of by Mr. Harington in his Analysis, by Mr. Beaufort in his Digest of the Criminal Law of Bengal, and by Mr. Baynes in his work on that of Madras. Some valuable works on both the civil and criminal codes of the Mohammadans have appeared in France, in Germany, in Holland, and at St. Petersburgh.

From this recapitulation it will be evident that a great want existed, and to some extent still exists of a standard authority for the elements of Mohammadan Law, and it was with a view to supply the defect that the late Sir William Macnaghten, when young in the Civil Service of the East India Company, undertook, as he expressly states, to furnish those whose duty it was to decide matters of civil controversy agreeably to the principles, in the first instance, of Mohammadan law, with the requisite practical information. Although a similar deficiency to a like extent was not attributable to the principles of Hindu law, yet there was an equal want of a general summary of its rudiments, that should obviate the necessity of reference to different and detached, and not always available, authorities, and for this therefore the same scholar undertook to provide. No individual in the service of the Company was equally competent to the task. Mr. Macnaghten came to India in the military branch of the service, and was an officer of cavalry on the Madras establishment; having obtained a civil appointment to Bengal he proceeded to Calcutta in 1814, and entered the College of that Presidency, where his Oriental studies were most successfully prosecuted. At the public Examination of the Students in August, 1815, the acting Visitor, the Honorable Mr. Edmonstone, in the absence of the Earl of Moira, took emphatic notice of his merits, announcing that subsequently to October in the previous year Mr. Macnaghten had gained Degrees of Honour in four languages, Arabic, Persian, Hindustani, and Bengali, and a medal of merit in a fifth, the Sanskrit. Upon leaving college he entered the judicial branch of the service, and was attached to the establishment of the Sadr Adálat in Calcutta, where he was occupied in translating and digesting the native documents brought forward by the suitors. In this position he did not relinquish his studies, but prosecuted the cultivation of Sanskrit and Arabic with reference particularly to the law literature of the

Hindus and Mohammadans, and after no very protracted interval passed an examination and gained prizes for his knowledge of both the language and the law in either department. Henceforth he devoted himself to the line he had chosen, and chiefly in connexion with the Sadr, of the proceedings of which court he published a series of valuable reports. Impressed with the want of available assistance towards a familiarity with the laws of both people as far as administered by the Company's Judges, he then compiled the Principles and Precedents, first of Mohammadan law, which was published at Calcutta in 1825, and next the Principles and Precedents of Hindu law, published at the same place in 1829. To the value of the latter, testimony of the highest description has been borne in the Judicial Committee of the Privy Council by Sir Edward Ryan, one of the Judges, and late Chief Judge of the Supreme Court of Calcutta, who stated that the work was all but decisive on any point of Hindu law contained in it, and that more respect would be paid to its dicta by the Judges of the Calcutta Board than even to the opinions of the Pandits.* A similar character is applicable to the Mohammadan portion.

The acknowledged value of Mr. Macnaghten's labours obviously recommended them as the best

* Moore's Indian Appeals, quoted by Morley, p. 239.

sources of the information that it is expected the candidates for the Civil Service of the Government of India shall acquire before leaving this country; especially as in addition to their authoritative character they are remarkable for clearness and concision, and are therefore peculiarly adapted to studies which are necessarily limited both as to time and scope. It has, therefore, been thought advisable to reprint the works, both of which are procurable with difficulty, if at all, in England, and permission to issue such a reprint has been liberally granted to me by the family of Sir William Macnaghten, whom I knew and esteemed throughout his career in Bengal, and whose melancholy and unmerited fate I have most sincerely regretted.

The original works of Mr. Macnaghten are entitled Principles and Precedents of Hindu and Mohammadan Law. The present publication is restricted to the Principles—the Precedents are cases decided upon, and illustrative of, the Principles, and are of unquestionable interest and importance; but for the reasons above intimated, the limitation of time, and the elementary nature of the knowledge to be acquired, it has been thought expedient to dispense on this occasion with the Precedents, as rendering the publication more extensive and elaborate than circumstances recommend. It may also be said of the Precedents, that their value is in some degree lessened by the subsequent multiplication of similar illustrations brought down to a much more recent date in Morley's Digest of Decisions, including the judgments of the Indian Courts to the year 1850; and by the Reported Decisions of the Sadr and Zila Courts of the three Presidencies, now published annually: still it will be highly advisable for the civilian, when actually engaged in the administration of justice in India, to provide himself with so safe and efficient a guide as Macnaghten's Principles and Precedents of Hindu and Mohammadan Law.

H. H. WILSON.

LONDON, *November*, 1859.

CONTENTS.

PRINCIPLES OF HINDU LAW.

PRINCIPLES OF MOHAMMADAN LAW.

CONTENTS.

PRINCIPLES OF HINDU LAW.

CHAPTER I.

OF PROPRIETARY RIGHT.

Property, according to the Hindu law, is of four descriptions, real, personal, ancestral, and acquired. I use the terms real and personal in preference to the terms moveable and immoveable, because, although the latter words would furnish a more strict translation of the expressions in the original, yet the Hindu law classes amongst things immoveable, property which is of an opposite nature, such as slaves and corrodies, or assignments on land.* In a work of this kind, intended solely for the purpose of practical utility, it would be useless to attempt any inquiry as to the origin of the right of property according to the notions of the Hindus, or as to the nature of the tenures of real property in India.

* *Jim. Va.* cited in Dig. vol. iii., page 34.

The various modes of acquisition, as occupancy, birth, gift, purchase, and the like, have been detailed and commented on with all the elaborate minuteness of the Hindu jurists.* It seems sufficient here to inquire into the nature of that property which is created by birth, for to this source must be traced all the impediments which exist to alienation; a man without heirs having an absolute and uncontrolled dominion over his property, by whatever means acquired. That an indefeasible, inchoate right is created by birth, seems to be universally admitted, though much argumentative discussion has been used to establish that this alone is not sufficient to create proprietary right. The most approved conclusion appears to be, that the inchoate right arising from birth, and the relinquishment by the occupant (whether effected by death or otherwise), conjointly create this right; the inchoate right which previously existed becoming perfected by the removal of the obstacle,† that is, by the death of the owner (natural or civil), or his voluntary abandonment.‡ In ancestral

* Is property included in the seven categories, substance and the rest, or is it distinct therefrom? *Jagannátha* in the Digest, vol. ii., p. 506; and ownership, in his opinion, following the *Nyáya* doctrine, "is a relation between cause and effect, attached to the owner who is predicated, of particular substances, and subsisting in the substance by connexion with the predicable."

† *Srikrishna*, cited in the Digest, vol. ii., p. 517.

‡ The fact of the ancestor being missing for a period exceeding twelve years, constitutes a legal title to succession on the part of the heirs. This doctrine was recognized in a case decided by the Sadr Diwání Adálat, on the 25th of April, 1820: Reports, vol. iii., page 28, wherein it was determined that twelve years should be allowed for the reappearance of the missing person, after which his death will be presumed, but some authorities maintain that the period varies with reference to the age of the missing person.

real property, the right is always limited; and the sons, grandsons, and great grandsons of the occupant, supposing them to be free from those defects, mental or corporeal, which are held to defeat the right of inheritance,* are declared to possess an interest in such property equal to that of the occupant himself; so much so, that he is not at liberty to alienate it, except under special and urgent circumstances, or to assign any larger share of it to one of his descendants than to another.† With respect to personal property of every description, whether ancestral or acquired, and with respect to real property acquired or recovered by the occupant, he is at liberty to make any alienation or distribution which he may think fit, subject only to spiritual responsibility.‡ The property of the father being thus restricted in respect of ancestral real property, and wills and testaments being wholly unknown to the Hindu law, it follows, for the sake of consistency, that

* Various diseases and various offences have been declared by the Hindu legislators to be of such a nature as to disqualify for inheritance. It is problematical how far our courts would go in support of objections which must in some instances be deemed irrational prejudices. The only reported case in which the question has been agitated, may be found in the Bengal Reports pages 108 and 257, vol. ii.; and in the Bombay Reports, p. 411, vol. i. There is a case reported, in which a widow's claim to her husband's estate was disallowed on account of her blindness. For an enumeration of the disqualifying causes, see Digest of Hindu law, p. 298, vol. iii., and Elem. Hin. Law, App., p. 335, *et seq.*; and the chapter vol. ii., treating of Exclusion from Inheritance, to the note in which an enumeration of the several disqualifying circumstances has been given. M.—Amongst them is the man who has been formally degraded or expelled by his kinsmen, p. 301. W.

† *Jagannátha*, in Dig. vol. iii., p. 45.

‡ *Vrihaspati*, in Dig. vol. iii., p. 32.

they must be wholly inoperative, and that their provisions must be set aside where they are at variance with the law; otherwise a person would be competent to make a disposition to take effect after his death, to which he could not have given effect during his lifetime.* A will is nothing more or less than "the legal declaration of a man's intentions, which he will to be performed after his death;" but willing to do that which the law has prohibited cannot be held to be a *legal* declaration of a man's intentions. There may be a gift in contemplation of death, but a will, in the sense in which it is understood in the English law, is wholly unknown to the Hindu system; and such gift can only be held valid under the same circumstances as those under which an ordinary gift would be considered valid. What may not be done *inter vivos*, may not be done by will. Of this description is the unequal distribution of ancestral real property. There are certain acts prohibited by the law, which, however, if carried into effect, cannot according to the law of Bengal be set aside, and which, though immoral, and in one sense of the word illegal, cannot be held to be invalid. For instance, a father, though declared to have absolute power

* For a more full discussion of the right of a Hindu to make a will, see Considerations on Hindu Law, p. 320, wherein the opinion of Mr. Colebrooke is introduced, to which the doctrine here laid down is conformable. See also the case of Hari Ballabh Gangaram, *v.* Keshoram Sheodas, Bombay Reports, vol. ii., p. 6, in which the plea of a will in opposition to the claims of heirs, was treated as inadmissible, and repugnant to the Hindu law, and the case of Sobharam Sambhúdas, *v.* Paramanand Bhaíchand, ibid., p. 471; also the case of Musst. Gúlâb, *v.* Musst. Phúl, vol. i., p. 154; and that of Gangaram Viswanâth, *v.* Tappi Baí, ibid., p. 372; and of Túljaram Hurjívan, *v.* Harbheram and another, ibid., p. 380; also App. Elem. Hin. Law, p. 9, *et passim*, and p. 405, *et seq.*

over property acquired by himself, is prohibited from making an unequal distribution of such property among his sons, by preferring one or excluding another without sufficient cause. This has been declared in the *Dáyabhága* to be a precept, not a positive law; and it is therein laid down that a gift or transfer under such circumstances is not null; "for a fact cannot be altered by a hundred texts." There is nothing inconsistent in this, as the doctrine is rather confirmatory of the texts which declare the absolute nature of the father's power over such property; but it has been held to extend to the legalizing of an unequal distribution of ancestral real property, and thereby interpreted in direct opposition to a positive law, which declares the ownership of the father and the son to be equal with respect to this description of property. But it cannot legitimately bear such a construction. It cannot be held to nullify an existing law, though it may be construed as declaring a precept inoperative with reference to the power expressly conferred by the law, or, in other words, to signify that an act may be legally right, though morally objectionable. Thus a coparcener is prohibited from disposing of his own share of joint ancestral property; and such an act, where the doctrine of the *Mitákshará* prevails (which does not recognize any several right until after partition, or the principle of *factum valet*), would undoubtedly be both illegal and invalid. But according to *Dáyabhága*, which recognizes this principle, and also a several though unascertained right in each coparcener, even before partition, a sale or other transfer under such circumstances would be valid and binding, as far as concerned the share of the transferring party. In the case of Bhawanípershad Goh, *versus* Musst. Taramaní, it was determined by the Sadr Diwání Adálat, that according to the Hindu law as current in Bengal, a coparcener may dispose of, by gift or otherwise, his own undivided share of the ancestral landed property, notwithstanding he may have a daughter and a daughter's son living; * while in the case of Nandram and others, it was determined that, according to the law as current in Behar, a gift of joint undivided property, whether real or personal, is not valid, even to the extent of the donor's own share.† I am aware that cases have been decided in opposition to the doctrine for which I here contend. These I propose briefly to notice. The first on record is that of Rasiklal Datt and Harilal Datt, executors of the will of Madanmohan Datt, *versus* Cheytancharn Datt, cited by Sir Thomas Strange, in his Elements of Hindu law.‡ He states, that the case was decided about the year 1789; that the testator, a Hindu, the father of four sons, and possessed of property of both descriptions, ancestral and self-acquired, having provided for his eldest by appointment, and advanced to the three younger ones in his life the means of their establishment, thought proper to leave the whole of what he possessed to the two younger ones, to the disherison of the two

* Sadr Diwání Adálat Reports, vol. iii., p. 138. The same doctrine was held in the case of Ramkanhai Rai and others, *v.* Bangchand Banhújea, ibid., 17, and the subject is more fully discussed by Mr. Colebrocke, in a note to vol. i., pp. 47 and 117.

† Case of Nandram and others, *v.* Kasi Pande and others, Sadr Diwání Adálat Reports, vol. iii., p. 232. The same doctrine was held in the case of Uman Datt, *v.* Kanhia Singh, ibid., 144.

‡ Vol. i., page 262.

elder, of whom the second disputed the will: that on reference to the pundits of the court, they affirmed the validity of the will, their answers being short; and that Sir W. Jones and Sir Robert Chambers concurred in this determination. The author of the Elements adds: "The ground with the pundits probably was (the Bengal maxim) that, however inconsistent the act with the ordinary rules of inheritance and the legal pretensions of the parties, *being done*, its validity was unquestionable." To this it can only be answered, that the motives which actuated the pundits in their exposition of the law, and the judges in their decision, are avowedly stated on conjecture only; and that if such motives are allowed to operate, there must be an end to all law, the maxim of *factum valet* superseding every doctrine and legalizing every act. The particulars of the case not having been stated, it cannot with safety be relied on as a precedent.

The second case is that of Ishanchand Rai *versus* Ishwarchand Rai, decided in the Sadr Diwání Adálat on the 23d of February 1792.* In that case it was held, that a gift, in the nature of a will, made by the *Zemindar* of Nadiya, settling the whole of his zemindarí on the eldest of his four sons, subject to a pecuniary provision for the younger ones, was good. The pundits are stated to have assigned six reasons for this opinion, not one of which, except the last, appears entitled to any weight. That last reason assigned, namely, that a principality may lawfully and properly be given to an eldest son, is doubtless correct, and

* Sadr Diwání Adálat Reports, vol. i., p.

taking a zemindarí in the light of a principality, is applicable, and would alone have sufficed to legalize the transaction.

A principality has indeed been enumerated among things impartible. But with respect to the other reasons assigned, they may be briefly replied to as follows. To the first that, "According to law, a present made by a father to his son, through affection, shall not be shared by the brethren," it may be objected, that this relates to property other than ancestral, over which the father is expressly declared to have control. To the second, "That what has been acquired by any of the enumerated lawful means, among which inheritance is one, is a fit subject of gift," that this supposes an acquisition in which no other person is entitled to participate, and not the case of an ancestral estate, in which the right of father and son has been declared equal. To the third, "That a coheir may dispose of his own share of undivided property," that his right to do so is admitted: but this does not include his right to alienate the shares of others. To the fourth, "That although a father be forbidden to give away lands, yet if he nevertheless do so, he merely sins, and the gift holds good," that the precept extends only to property over which the father has absolute authority, and cannot affect the law, which expressly declares him to have no greater interest than his son in the ancestral estate. And to the fifth, "That *Raghunandana* in the *Dáyatatwa*, restricting a father from giving lands to one of his sons, but clothes and ornaments only, is at variance with *Jimutavahana*, whose doctrine he espouses, and who only says that a father acts blamably in so doing," that no such variance really exists. In addition to the above, it may be stated, that the suit in question was brought by an uncle against his nephew, to recover a portion of an estate which had previously devolved entire on the brother of the claimant, and which, it appeared, had never been divided.*

The third case is that of Ramkúmar Nyaya Bachespatí, *versus* Kishenkinker Tarka Bhúshan decided by the Sadr Diwání Adálat on the 24th of November, 1812.† In that case it was maintained, that the gift by a father of the whole ancestral estate to one son, to the prejudice of the rest, or even to a stranger, is a valid act, (although an immoral one,) according to the doctrine received in Bengal. To refute the opinion declared by the pundits on that occasion, it is merely necessary to state the authorities quoted by them, which would have been more applicable to the maintenance of the opposite doctrine. The following were the authorities cited in support of the above opinion. 1st. The text of *Vishnu* cited in the *Dáyabhága*: "When a father separates his sons from himself, his will regulates the division of his own acquired wealth." 2nd. A quotation also from the *Dáyabhága*: "The father has ownership in gems, pearls, and other moveables, though inherited from the grandfather, and not recovered by him, just as in his own acquisitions; and has power to distribute them unequally; as *Yájnyawalkya* intimates: 'The father is master of the gems, pearls and corals, and of all (other moveable property): but neither the father nor the grandfather is

* See Appendix Elem. Hin. Law, p. 437.
† Sadr Diwání Adálat Reports, vol. ii., p. 42.

so of the whole immoveable estate.' Since the grandfather is here mentioned, the text must relate to his effects. By again saying, 'all' after specifying 'gems, pearls,' etc., it is shown, that the father has authority to make a gift or any similar disposition of all effects, other than land, etc. but not of immoveables, a corrody, and chattels, (*i. e.* slaves); since here also it is said 'the whole,' this prohibition forbids the gift or other alienation of the whole, because (immoveable and similar possessions are) means of supporting the family. For the maintenance of the family is an indispensable obligation, as *Manu* positively declares: 'The support of persons who should be maintained, is the approved means of attaining heaven: but hell is the man's portion if they suffer.' Therefore (let a master of a family) carefully maintain them. The prohibition is not against a donation or other transfer of a small part, not incompatible with the support of the family: for the insertion of the word 'whole' would be unmeaning, (if the gift of even a small part were forbidden)." The text of *Yájnyawalkya* cited in the *Prayashchitta-vivek:* "From the non-performance of acts which are enjoined, from the commission of acts which are declared to be criminal, and from not exercising a control over the passions, a man incurs punishment in the next world." An examination of the authorities above quoted, as given by the law officers in the case in question, will make it evident that they are totally insufficient for the support of the doctrine to which they were intended to apply.

The fourth case is that of Sham Singh, *versus* Musst. Amraotí, decided in the Sadr Diwání Adálat on the 28th of July, 1813,* on which occasion it was determined, that, by the Hindu law as current in Mithilá, a father cannot give away the whole ancestral property to one son to the exclusion of his other sons. The author of the Considerations on Hindu Law, commenting on this decision, infers that the Sadr Diwání Adálat would not have entertained any doubt as to the validity of the gift, had it depended upon the law as current in Bengal; but there seems to be no other ground for this inference than the erroneous doctrines laid down in the two previously cited cases, together with the fact of the parties having disputed as to which law should govern the decision.

The fifth case is that of Bhawanicharan Banhújea, *versus* the heirs of Ramkant Banhújea, which was decided in the Sadr Diwání Adálat on the 27th of December 1816,† and in which case it was ruled, that an unequal distribution made by a father among his sons of ancestral immoveable property is illegal and invalid, as is also the unequal distribution of property acquired by the father, and of moveable ancestral property, if made under the influence of a motive which is held in law to deprive a person of the power to make a distribution. The question as to the father's power was thoroughly investigated on this occasion. There being a difference of opinion between the pundits attached to the Sadr Diwání Adálat, the following question was proposed to the pundits of the Supreme Court, Tarapershad and Mrityúnjayí, to Narahari, pundit

* Sadr Diwání Adálat Reports, vol. ii., p. 74.
† Sadr Diwání Adálat Reports, vol. ii., p. 202.

of the Calcutta provincial court, and Ramajaya, a pundit attached to the College of Fort William: "A person whose elder son is alive, makes a gift to his younger, of all his property, moveable and immoveable, ancestral and acquired. Is such a gift valid, according to the law authorities current in Bengal, or not? and if it be invalid, is it to be set aside?"

The following answer, under the signatures of the four pundits above mentioned, was received to this reference:—"If a father, whose elder son is alive, make a gift to his younger, of all his acquired property, moveable and immoveable, and of all the ancestral moveable property, the gift is valid, but the donor acts sinfully. If during the lifetime of an elder son, he make a gift to his younger, of all the ancestral immoveable property, such gift is not valid. Hence, if it have been made, it must be set aside. The learned have agreed that it must be set aside, because such a gift is *à fortiori* invalid: inasmuch as he (the father) cannot even make an unequal distribution among his sons of ancestral immoveable property; as he is not master of all; as he is required by law, even against his own will, to make a distribution among his sons of ancestral property not acquired by himself (*i. e.* not recovered); as he is incompetent to distribute such property among his sons until the mother's courses have ceased, lest a son subsequently born should be deprived of his share; and as, while he has children living, he has no authority over the ancestral property.

"Authorities in support of the above opinions. 1st. *Vishnu*, cited in the *Dáyabhága*:—'He regulates the division of his own acquired wealth.' 2nd. *Yájnyawalkya*, cited in the *Dáyabhága* :—'The father is master of the gems, pearls, corals and of all other moveable property.' 3rd. *Dáyábhága* :—'The father has ownership in gems, pearls, and other moveables, though inherited from the grandfather, and not recovered by him, just as in his own acquisitions.' 4th. *Dáyabhága*: 'But not so, if it were immoveable property inherited from the grandfather, because they have an equal right to it. The father has not in such case an unlimited discretion.' Unlimited discretion is interpreted by *Srikrishna Tarkalankára* to signify a competency of disposal at pleasure. 5th. *Dáyabhága* :—'Since the circumstance of the father being lord of all the wealth is stated as a reason, and that cannot be in regard to the grandfather's estate, an unequal distribution made by the father is lawful only in the instance of his own acquired wealth.' Commentary of Srikrishna on the above texts:—'Although the father be in truth lord of all the wealth inherited from ancestors, still the right here meant is not merely ownership, but competency for disposing of the wealth at pleasure; and the father has not such full dominion over property ancestral.' 6th. *Dáyabhága* : 'If the father recover paternal wealth seized by strangers, and not recovered by other sharers, nor by his own father, he shall not, unless willing, share it with his sons; for in fact it was acquired by him.' In this passage, *Manu* and *Vishnu* declaring that 'he shall not, unless willing, share it, because it was acquired by himself,' seem thereby to intimate a partition amongst sons, even against the father's will, in the case of hereditary wealth not acquired (that is, recovered) by him. 7th. *Dáyabhága*:—'When the mother is past child-bearing,' regards wealth inherited from the paternal grandfather. Since other children cannot be borne by her when her courses have ceased, partition among sons may then take place; still, however by the choice of the father. But if the hereditary estate were divided while she continued to be capable of child-bearing, those born subsequently would be deprived of subsistence: neither would that be right; for a text expresses: 'They who are born, and they who are yet unbegotten, and they who are actually in the womb, all require the means of support; and the dissipation of their hereditary maintenance is censured.' *Srikrishna* has interpreted 'the dissipation of hereditary maintenance' to signify, the being deprived of a share in the ancestral wealth. 8th. *Dwaitanirnaya*: 'If there be offspring, the parents have no authority over the ancestral wealth; and from the declaration of their having no authority, any unauthorized act committed by them is invalid.' 9th. Text of *Vijnyáneswara*, cited in the scholia of Medhatithi:—'Let the judge declare void a sale without ownership, and a gift or pledge unauthorized by the owner.' The term 'without ownership,' intends incompetency of disposal at pleasure. 10th. Text of *Náreda*:—'That act which is done by an infant, or by any person not possessing authority, must be considered as not done. The learned in the law have so declared.'"

I have given the above opinion, together with the authorities cited in its support, at full length, from its being apparently the most satisfactory doctrine hitherto recorded on the subject. By declaring void any illegal alienation of the ancestral real property, it preserves the law from the imputation of being a dead letter, and protects the son from being deprived by the caprice of the father, of that in which the law has repeatedly and expressly declared them both to have equal ownership. The case of Ramkant is the latest reported decision by the Sadr Diwání Adálat connected with the point in question. Various cases have been cited by the author of the "Considerations,"* in which wills made by Hindus have been upheld by the Supreme Court, though at variance with the doctrine above laid down. The will of Raja Nobkishen, who, although he had a begotten and an adopted son, left an ancestral *talúk* to the sons of his brother, is perhaps the most remarkable of the cases cited; but in this, as well as in most of the others, the point of law was never touched upon, the parties having joined issue on questions of fact. Upon the whole, I conclude that the text of the *Dáyabhága*, which is the groundwork of all the doubts and perplexity that have been raised on this question, can merely be held to confer a legal power of alienating property, where such power is not expressly taken away by some other text. Thus in Bengal, a man may make an unequal distribution among his sons of his personally acquired property, or of the ancestral moveable property; because, though it has been enjoined† to a father not to distinguish one son at a partition made in his lifetime, nor on any account to exclude one from participation without sufficient

* See the chapter on Wills, p. 316 *et passim.*

† *Katyáyana*, cited in Dig., vol. ii., p. 540.

cause, yet as it has been declared in another place that the father is master of all moveable property, and of his own acquisitions,* the maxim that a fact cannot be altered by a hundred texts here applies to legalize a disregard of the injunction, there being texts declaratory of unlimited discretion, of equal authority with those which condemn the practice.† In other parts of India, where the maxim in question does not obtain, the injunction applies in its full force, and any prohibited alienation would be considered illegal.‡ The subject will be resumed in the chapter treating of partition.

* *Yájnyawalkya*, ibid., p. 159.

† Elem. Hin. Law, vol. i., p. 123, and App. Chap. 1st, and see Bombay Reports, pp. 154, 372, and 380, vol. i., and pp. 6 and 471, vol. ii.

‡ The latest authority on the subject of wills made by Hindus is to be found in Morley's Digest of Reported cases; vol. i., p. 612, note; where, after stating the opinions of Mr. Colebrooke and Sir Francis Macnaghten, he concludes: "The wills of Hindus have been recognized in the Courts of the Honorable Company in all the Presidencies, with the restriction that the testators cannot bequeath property which they were incompetent to alienate during their life time." W.

CHAPTER II.

OF INHERITANCE.

ACCORDING to the Hindu law of inheritance, as it at present exists, all legitimate sons, living in a state of union with their father at the time of his death, succeed equally to his property, real and personal, ancestral and acquired. In former times, the right of primogeniture prevailed to a certain extent; but that, with other usages, has been abrogated in the present or

* See the case Taliwar Sing, *versus* Pahlwan Sing, Sadr Diwání Adálat Reports, vol. iii. p. 203, wherein a claim of primogeniture being preferred, it was determined that priority of birth does not entitle to a larger portion. There is another decision on record (vol. ii., p. 116) of a case in which there were sons by different wives, and one party claimed that the estate should be distributed according to the number of wives, without reference to the number of sons borne by each, (a distribution technically termed *Patnibhága*,) averring that such had been the *Kuláchár*, or immemorial usage of the family; but the Court determined that the distribution among them should be made, not with reference to the mothers, but with reference to the number of sons; being of opinion, that although, in cases of inheritance, *Kuláchár*, or family

Kali age.* The right of representation is also admitted, as far as the great-grandson: and the grandson and great-grandson, the father of the one and the father and grandfather of the other being dead, will take equal shares with their uncle and grand-uncle respectively. Indeed the term *putra* or son, has been held to signify, in its strict acceptation, a grandson and great-grandson. An adopted son is a substitute for a son of the body, where none such exists, and is entitled to the same rights and privileges. Among the sons of the *Sudra* tribe, an illegitimate son by a slave girl takes with his legitimate brothers a half share; and where there are no sons (including son's sons and grandsons), but only the son of a daughter, he is considered as a co-heir, and takes an equal share.*

In default of sons, the grandsons inherit, in which case they take *per stirpes,* the sons, however numerous, of one son, taking no more than the sons, however few, of another son.

In default of sons and grandsons, the great-grandsons inherit; in which case they also take *per stirpes,* the sons,

usage, has the prescriptive force of law; yet, to establish *Kuláchár,* it is necessary that the usage have been ancient and invariable. See also the case of Bhyrochand Rai, *versus* Rassikmaní, vol. i., p. 27, and the case of Sheo Baksh Sing, *versus* the heir of Futteh Sing, vol. ii., p. 265. See also Elem. Hin. Law, App. p. 288. In the succession to principalities and large landed possessions, long established *Kuláchár* will have the effect of law, and convey the property to one son to the exclusion of the rest. It has been stated by Mr. Colebrooke, in a note to the Digest (vol. ii., p. 119), that the great possessions called *zemindaris* in official language, are considered by modern Hindu lawyers as tributary principalities.

* Mitákshará, Chap. i. Sect. xii. §§ 1 and 2.

however numerous, of one grandson taking no more than the sons, however few, of another grandson. They will take the shares to which their respective fathers would have been entitled had they survived.

In default of sons, grandsons, and great-grandsons in the male line, the inheritance descends lineally no farther, and the widow inherits, according to the law as current in Bengal, whether her late husband was separated, or was living as a member of an undivided family; but according to other schools, the widow succeeds to the inheritance in the former case only, an undivided brother being held to be the next heir. If there be more than one widow, their rights are equal.* Much discussion has arisen respecting the nature of the tenure by which a widow holds property that had devolved upon her by the death of her husband; and certainly the law, in this instance, as in many others, admits of great latitude of interpretation. It is well known, that between the Bengal and the other schools, there is a difference of opinion as to the circumstances under which a widow has a right to succeed to the property of the deceased husband. By the law as current in Bengal, as has been already observed, she is entitled to succeed, whether the husband was living in a state of union with, or separation from, his brethren. By that of other schools, only where the husband was separated from his brethren. So far, as to the right of succession, the law is clear and indisputable; but to what

* See Elem. Hin. Law, App. p. 59.

she succeeds is not so apparent. She has not an absolute proprietary right, neither can she, in strictness, be called even a tenant for life: for the law provides her successors, and restricts her use of the property to very narrow limits. She cannot dispose of the smallest part, except for necessary purposes, and certain other objects particularly specified. It follows, then, that she can be considered in no other light than as a holder in trust for certain uses; so much so, that should she make waste, they who have the reversionary interest have clearly a right to restrain her from so doing. What constitutes waste, however, must be determined by the circumstances of each individual case. The law has not defined the limits of her discretion with sufficient accuracy, and it was probably never in the contemplation of the legislator that the widow should live apart from, and out of the personal control of, her husband's relations or possess the ability to expend more than they might deem right and proper. In assigning a motive for the ordinance that a widow should succeed to her husband, and at the same time that she should be deprived of the advantages enjoyed by a tenant for life even, it seems most consistent with probability that it originated in a desire to secure against all contingencies, a provision for the helpless widow, and thereby prevent her from having recourse to practices by which the fame and honour of the family might be tarnished. By giving her a nominal property, she acquires consideration and respectability, and by making her the depositary of the wealth, she is guarded against the neglect or cruelty of her husband's relations.

At the same time, by limiting her power a barrier is raised against the effects of female improvidence and worldly inexperience. This opinion receives corroboration from the distinction which prevails in the Benares school, which may be said to be the fountain and source of all Hindu law. By the provisions of that code, where the brothers are united with the deceased husband, and where consequently it is fair to presume a spirit of friendship and cordiality, and there is no reason to anticipate that the widow will be treated with neglect by the brothers, she is declared to have no right of succession. It is only where the family is divided, and where there might consequently be reason to apprehend a want of brotherly feeling, that the law deems it necessary to interpose and protect her interests. And it may be here observed, that if a man die leaving more than one widow, (three widows, for instance,) the property is considered as vesting in only one individual: thus, on the death of one or two of the widows the survivor or survivors take the property, and no part vests in the other heirs of the husband until after the death of all the widows.

According to the doctrine of the *Smriti Chandriká*, which is of great and paramount authority in the south of India, a widow, being the mother of daughters, takes her husband's property, both moveable and immoveable, where the family is divided; but a childless widow takes only the moveable property. Where there are two widows, one the mother of daughters and the other childless, the former alone takes the immoveable estate, and the moveable property is equally divided between them.

In default of the widow, the daughter inherits, but neither is her interest absolute. According to the doctrine of the Bengal school, the unmarried daughter is first entitled to the succession: if there be no maiden daughter, then the daughter who has, and the daughter who is likely to have, male issue are together entitled to the succession;* and on failure of either of them, the other takes the heritage. Under no circumstances can the daughters, who are either barren, or widows destitute of male issue, or the mothers of daughters only, inherit the property.

But there is a difference in the law, as it obtains in Benares, on this point, that school holding that a maiden is in the first instance entitled to the property; failing her, that the succession devolves on the married daughters who are indigent, to the exclusion of the wealthy daughters; that, in default of indigent daughters, the wealthy daughters are competent to inherit; but no preference is given to a daughter who has or is likely to have male issue, over a daughter who is barren, or a childless widow.

According to the law of Mithilá, an unmarried daughter is preferred to one who is married: failing her, married

* A distinction is made by *Srikrishna*, in his commentary on the *Dáyabhága*, in respect of unmarried daughters. He is of opinion, that the daughter who is not betrothed is first entitled to the inheritance; and in her default the daughter who is betrothed; but this doctrine is not concurred in by any other authority, and the author of the *Dáyarahasya* expressly impugns it as untenable.

daughters are entitled to the inheritance; but there is no distinction made among the married daughters; and one who is married, and has or is likely to have male issue, is not preferred to one who is widowed and barren; nor is there any distinction made between indigence and wealth.

It may here be mentioned, that the above rule of succession is applicable to Bengal in every possible case; but, elsewhere, only where the family is divided: for according to the doctrine of the Benares and other schools, even the widow, to whom the daughter is postponed, can never inherit, where the family is in a state of union; nor can the mother, daughter, daughter's son, or grandmother. The father's heirs in such case exclude them. But though the schools differ on these points, they concur in opinion as to the manner in which such property devolves on the daughter's death, in default of issue male. According to the law as received in Benares and elsewhere, it does not go as her *Stridhan*, to her husband or other heir; and according to the law of Bengal also, it reverts to her father's heirs.* In the case of Rajchandra Das, *versus* Dhanmaní, it was determined, that according to the Hindu law as current in Bengal, on the death of a widow who had claimed her husband's

* It has been asserted by the author of the Elements of Hindu Law, p. 161, that property, devolved on a daughter by inheritance, is classed by the southern authorities as *Stridhan*, and descends accordingly. The authority cited for this doctrine is to be found in that part of the Mitákshará treating of women's peculiar property, and consequently applies to the descent of that alone. I have not been able to meet with any other.

property, her daughter will inherit, to the exclusion of her husband's brother, if the daughter has or is likely to have male issue: and on her death without issue, her father's brother will inherit, to the exclusion of her husband.* But a curious case arose at Bombay,† involving the daughter's right, which deserves notice in this place. Of two widows one had two sons, and the other a daughter. On the death of the latter widow it became a question who was to succeed to her property, whether her daughter or the rival widow's sons. Various authorities were consulted, and they inclined to the opinion, that the daughter was not entitled to succeed as heir, inasmuch as property which had devolved on a widow, reverts at her death to her husband's heirs, among whom the daughter would have ranked, in default only of her own brothers.

According to the law of Bengal and Benares, the daughter's sons inherit, in default of the qualified daughters: but the right of daughter's sons is not recognised by the Mithilá school. If there be sons of more than one daughter, they take *per capita*, and not as the son's sons do *per stirpes*.‡ If one of several daughters.

* Sadr Diwáni Adálat Reports, vol. iii., p. 362.

† Elem. Hin. Law, App. p. 392.

‡ The same author states, p. 160, that "where such sons are numerous, when they do take, they take *per stirpes*, and not *per capita*." But the reverse of this is proved by the authority cited in its favour, Dig. vol. iii., p. 501. *Jagannátha* there lays down the following rule: "Again, if daughter's sons be numerous, a distribution must be made. In that case, if there be two sons of one daughter, and three of another, five equal shares must be allotted: they shall not first divide the estate in two parts,

who had, as maidens, succeeded to their father's property, die leaving sons and sisters, or sisters' sons, then, according to the law of Bengal the sons alone take the share to which the mother was entitled, to the exclusion of the sisters and the sisters' sons;* and if one of several daughters, who had as married women, succeeded their father, die leaving sons, sisters, or sisters' sons, according to the same law the sisters exclude the sons: and if there be no sister, the property will be equally shared by her sons and her sisters' sons. This distinction does not seem to prevail anywhere but in Bengal. The author of the Considerations on Hindu Law has stated the following case:—"If there be three sisters who succeed jointly to their father's estate, A, B, and C, and supposing A to die childless, and B and C to survive her. Supposing also B to have one son, and C to have three sons, and supposing C to have died before A, and B to have survived her; it is agreed, that upon the death of A, her estate will go to B; but whether on the death of B, it shall go to her *only* son, or be divided between him and the three sons of C, is *vexata quaestio.*" In this case I apprehend, that if the property had devolved on the

and afterwards allot one share to each son." This principle was maintained also in the case of Ramdhan Sen and others *v.* Kishenkant Sen and others, it being therein determined, that grandsons by different mothers claiming their maternal grandfather's property take *per capita*, and not *per stirpes*. Sadr Diwání Adálat Reports, vol. iii., p. 100.

* Conformably to this doctrine, a case which originated in the *zillah* court of Rungpore was decided by the Sadr Diwání Adálat, on the 19th of April, 1820, in which it was determined (see Reports, vol. ii., p. 26) that property inherited by a daughter goes at her death to her son or grandson, to the exclusion of her sister and sister's son.

daughters at the time they were maidens, then on C's death her property would go to her three sons, and not to her sisters; but if they were married at the time, it would go to her sisters; and on the death of A, to B; and on the death of B, her sons and the sons of B would take *per capita*, and this upon the general principle, that property which had devolved on a daughter is taken at her death by the heirs of her father, and not by the heirs of the daughter, and the father's heirs in this case are his daughter's sons, who are entitled to equal shares.* Under no circumstances can a daughter's son's son or other descendant, or her daughter or husband, inherit immediately from her the property which devolved on her at her father's death: such property, according to the tenets of all the schools, will devolve on her father's next heir, and will not go as her *Stridhan*, to her own heir.

In default of daughter's sons, the father inherits, according to the law as current in Bengal; but according to other schools,† the mother succeeds to the exclusion of the father.

* *Jim. Vah.* in the *Dáyabhága*, chap. xi. sec. i., § 65. II.—See Case 5. Chap. Rights of Daughters, etc., vol. ii.

† According to the doctrine of *Jimútavahana* and others, whose works are current in Bengal, the mother's right of succession is admitted after the father. *Jimútavahana* says, that "in the term *pitarau*" both parents (contained in the text of *Yájnyawalkya*, vide Dáyabhága, p. 160) "the priority of the father is indicated: for the father is first suggested by the radical term *pitri;* and afterwards the mother is inferred from the dual number, by assuming, that one term (of two which composed the phrase) is retained." But the followers of the schools of Benares and Mithilá give the mother the preference over the father, as will more clearly

In default of the father, the mother inherits. Her interest, however, is not absolute, and is of a nature similar to that of a widow. In a case of property which had devolved on a mother by the decease of her son, the law officers of the Sadr Diwání Adálat held that the rules

appear from the subjoined extract containing the doctrine on this subject of the *Mitákshará*, with Mr. Colebrooke's remarks. "Therefore, since the mother is the nearest of the two parents, it is most fit that she should take the estate. But, on failure of her, the father is successor to the property." The commentator, *Bálambhatta*, is of opinion, that the father should inherit first, and afterwards the mother; upon the analogy of more distant kindred, where the paternal line has invariably the preference before the maternal kindred; and upon the authority of several passages of law, *Nandapandita*, author of commentaries on the *Mitákshará* and on the institutes of *Vishnu*, had before maintained the same opinion. But the elder commentator of the *Mitákshará*, *Vishweshwarabhatta*, has in this instance followed the text of his author in his own treatise entitled *Madanapárijáta*, and has supported *Vijnyaneswara's* argument, both there and in his commentary named *Subodhini*. Much diversity of opinion does indeed prevail on this question. *Sridhara* maintains, that the father and mother inherit together: and the great majority of writers of eminence (as *Aparárka* and *Kamalákára*, and the authors of the *Smritichandriká*, *Madanaratna*, *Vyavahára Mayûk'ha*, etc.) gives the father the preference before the mother. *Jimûtavahana* and *Raghunandana* have adopted this doctrine. But *Vácheaspatimisra*, on the contrary, concurs with the *Mitákshará* in placing the mother before the father; being guided by an erroneous reading of the text of *Vishnu*, as is remarked in the *Viramitrodaya*. The author of the latter work proposes to reconcile these contradictions by a personal distinction. "If the mother be individually more venerable than the father, she inherits; if she be less so, the father takes the inheritance."

The following is an extract from the *Vivádabhangárnava*: "More arguments might be brought to prove the pre-eminence of the mother; for example, her importance declared in an authoritative text: 'A mother surpasses a thousand fathers, for she bears and nourishes the child in the womb; therefore is a mother most venerable.'"

"If the veneration due to her exceed the respect due to a father a thousand fold, how can the text cited from the *Purána* by *Mádhavácharya* be relevant?"

"By law, the father and the mother are two reverend parents of a concerning property devolving on a widow equally affect property devolving on a mother.* On her death, the property devolves on the heirs of her son, and not on her heirs.

In default of father and mother, brothers inherit: first, the uterine associated brethren; next the unassociated brethren of the whole blood; thirdly, the associated brethren of the half blood: and fourthly, the unassociated brethren of the half blood. The above order supposes that

man in this world; however adorable *the goddess* of the earth, a mother is *still* more venerable. But, of these two, the father is pre-eminent, because the seed is chiefly considered; on failure of him, the mother is *most reverend*; after her the eldest brother."

"He himself thus reconciles the seeming contradiction: this relates to a father, *who gives instruction to his son in the whole Veda*, after performing the ceremonies on conception, and all other holy rites which perfect the twice-born man: otherwise the mother is most venerable. Accordingly the text of *Manu* is also pertinent."

Manu: "A mere Achárya, or a teacher of the *Gayatri only*, surpasses ten *Upádhyayás*; a father, a hundred such *acháryas*, and a mother a thousand natural fathers."

Vyása: "Ten months a mother bore her infant in her womb, suffering extreme anguish; fainting with travail and various pangs, she brought forth her child; loving her sons more than her life, the tender mother is *justly* revered; who could recite all her merits, even though he spoke a hundred years?"

"By citing other texts from the *Purános* the volume would be unnecessarily enlarged; for this reason they are omitted. The seeming difficulty is thus reconciled: title to respect is no cause of inheritance; were it so, who could take the estate, while both parents exist? But benefits conferred by his own act, and near relation by the funeral cake, *are the grounds on which rest the claim of an heir.* Now the father is superior by the benefits which he confers: therefore he has the right of succession, even though the mother be living."

But although a great majority of writers gives the father the preference over the mother, yet according to the law as current in Benares and Mithilá, the mother has the superior claim of inheritance.

* Case of Musst. Bijia Dibia *v.* Annapúrna Dibia, S. D. A. Reports, vol. i., p. 164.

the deceased had only uterine or only half brothers, and that they were all united or all separated. But if a man die, leaving an uterine brother separated and a half brother associated or re-united, these two will inherit the property in equal shares. Sisters are not enumerated in the order of heirs.

In a case recently decided in the Sadr Diwání Adálat, a question arose as to the relative rights of a brother and a brother's son to succeed, on the death of a widow, to property which had devolved on her at the death of her husband, they being the next heirs. The Pandits at first declared, that a brother's son (his father being dead) was entitled to inherit together with the brother. But this opinion was subsequently proved and admitted to be erroneous. In the succession to the estate of a grandfather, the right of representation undoubtedly exists; that is to say, the son of a deceassd son inherits together with his uncle: not so in the case of property left by a brother, the brother's son being enumerated in the order of heirs to a childless person's estate after the brother, and entitled to succeed only in default of the latter. In the case in question, the deceased left two brothers and a widow, and the widow succeeding, one of the brothers died during the time she held possession. The son of the brother who so died claimed, on the death of the widow, to inherit together with his uncle, and the fallacy of the opinion which maintained the justice of his claim consisted in supposing, that on the death of the first brother the right of inheritance of his other two surviving brothers immediately accrued, and that the dormant right of the brother who died secondly was transmitted to his son. But, in point of fact, while the widow survived, neither brother had even an inchoate right to inherit the property, and consequently the brother who died during her lifetime could not have transmitted to his son a right which never appertained to himself.*

In default of brothers, their sons inherit in the same order: but in regard to their succession, there is this peculiarity, that if a brother's sons, whose father died previously to the devolution of the property, claim by right of representation, they take *per stirpes* with their uncle, being in that case grandsons inheriting with a son; but when the succession devolves on the brother's sons alone as nephews, they take place *per capita*, as daughter's sons do. In the *Subodhini* it is stated, that the succession cannot, under any circumstances, take place *per capita*, but this opinion is overruled. He maintains also, that daughters of brothers inherit. In this opinion he is joined by *Nanda Pandita*, but the doctrine is elsewhere universally rejected. †

In default of brother's sons, their grandsons inherit in the same order, and in the same manner,‡ according

* Case of Rúdrachandra Chowdhri *v.* Sambhú Chandrachowdhry, Sadr Diwání Adálat Reports, vol. iii., p. 106. The same doctrine was maintained in the case of Musst. Jymaní Dibia *versus* Ramjog Chowdhi, ibid. 289.

† See note to Colebrooke's *Dáyabhága*, p. 348.

‡ It may here be observed, however, that no re-union after separation can take place with a grandson's brother. Re-union can take place only with the following relations: the father, the brother, and the paternal uncle. *Vrihaspati*, cited in the *Dáyabhága*, chap. xi., sec. 1, §. 30.

to the law as current in Bengal; but the law of Benares, Mithilá, and other provinces, does not enumerate the brother's grandson in the order of heirs, and assigns to the paternal grandmother the place next to the brother's son.

In default of brother's grandsons, sisters' sons inherit, according to the law of Bengal; but according to other schools, the paternal grandmother, as above stated, is ranked next to the brother's son, and the sister's son also is excluded from the enumerated heirs. This point of law was established in a case decided by the Sadr Adálat, in which the suit being for the landed estate of a deceased Hindu, situated in Bengal, by the son of his sister against the son of his paternal uncle, it was ruled, that according to the law of Bengal, the plaintiff would be heir, but according to the law of Mithilá the defendant.*

There is a difference of opinion among different writers of the Bengal school as to the whole and half blood; some maintaining that an uterine sister's son excludes the son of a sister of the half blood: but according to the most approved authorities, there should be no distinction. A sister's daughter is nowhere enumerated in the order of heirs.†

In default of sisters' sons, the inheritance is thus con-

* Case of Rajchandra Nárain *v.* Gokulchandra Goh, S. Diwání Adálat Reports, vol. i., p. 43. See also case 6, p. 125, vol. ii.

† *Nanda Pandita* and *Bálambhatta* maintain, that the daughters also of sisters have a right of inheritance: but their opinion is universally rejected on this point. See note to Colebrooke's *Dáyabhága*, page 348. See also a case reported in Appendix Elem. Hin. Law, page 249.

tinued agreeably to the doctrine of the Bengal school, as laid down in the *Dáyakramasangraha.* Brother's daughter's son — Paternal grandfather — Paternal grandmother—Paternal uncle, his son and grandson—Paternal grandfather's daughter's son—Paternal uncle's daughter's son—Paternal great-grandfather—Paternal great-grandmother—Paternal grandfather's brother, his son and grandson—Paternal great-grandfather's daughter's son, and his brother's daughter's son. On failure of all these, the inheritance goes in the maternal line to the maternal grandfather;* the maternal uncle; his son and grandson, and daughter's son; the maternal great-grandfather, his son, grandson, great grandson, and daughter's son; and to the maternal great-great-grandfather, his son, grandson, great-grandson, and daughter's son. In default of all these, the property goes to the remote kindred in the descending and ascending line, as far as the fourteenth in degree; then to the spiritual preceptor; the pupil; the fellow student;† those bearing the same name; those descended from the same patriarch;‡ Brahmins learned

* It has been remarked by *Jagannátha* (page 530, vol. iii.): "That the son of a son's and of a grandson's daughter, and the son of a brother's and of a nephew's daughter, and so forth, claim succession in the order of proximity, before the maternal grandfather;" but this opinion does not seem to be supported by any authority.

† See a Bombay case cited in Elem. Hin. Law, App. p. 257, in which it was determined, that a fellow hermit is heir to an anchoret; his pupil to an *ascetic*; and his preceptor to a professed student of theology.

‡ In some parts of India, especially in the south, there are Brahman families who claim to descend from celebrated saints and sages as from Bharadwaja, Gotama and others: in such case the individual is said to belong to the Gotra of the saint. W.

in the *Vedas;* and lastly, to the king, to whom, however, the property of a Brahmin can never escheat, but must be distributed among other Brahmins.

The above order of succession, however, is by no means universally adhered to, even among the writers of the Bengal school. After the sister's son, *Srikrishna Tarkálankára*, in his commentary on the *Dáyabhága*, places the paternal uncle of the whole blood; the son of the paternal uncle of the half blood; their grandsons successively; the paternal grandfather's daughter's son; the paternal grandfather; the paternal grandmother; the paternal grandfather's uterine brother; his half brother; their sons and grandsons successively; the paternal great-grandfather's daughter's son; the *Sapindas;* the maternal uncle and the rest, who present oblations which the deceased was bound to offer; the mother's sister's son; the maternal uncle's sons and grandsons; the grandson of the son's son, and other descendants for three generations in succession; the offspring of the paternal grandfather's grandfather, and other ancestors for three generations; the *Samánodakas* (those connected by obsequial offerings of water); and lastly, the spiritual teacher, etc., etc.

The series of heirs is thus stated by the compilers of the *Vivádárnavasetu* and *Vivádabhangárnava.** After the sister's son, the grandfather, next the grandmother: and afterwards the enumeration proceeds as follows. Uncle—

* Among modern digests, the most remarkable are the *Vivádárnavasetu*, compiled by order of Mr. Hastings; *Vivádasárárnava*, compiled at the request of Sir William Jones; and the *Vivádabhangárnava*, by *Jagannátha*. —Colebrooke's Preface to Digest, p. 23.

uncle's son—Grandson, and great grandson—Grandfather's daughter's son—Great-grandfather—Great-grandmother—Their son, grandson, great-grandson, and daughter's son—Maternal grandfather—Maternal uncle, his son, and grandson—The deceased's grandson's grandson (in the male line), his great-grandson, and his great-great-grandson. Then the ascending line succeed, namely, the paternal great-grandfather's father, his son, grandson, and great-grandson.*

The above cited four authorities are of the greatest weight in the province of Bengal; and where they differ, reliance may with safety be placed on the *Dáyakramasangraha* of *Srikrishna*.† It will be observed, however, that all these authorities concur in the order of enumeration as far as the sister's son, which perhaps is all that will be requisite for practical purposes; and it would be but waste of time to enter into any disquisition as to the differences of opinion entertained by writers of inferior importance.

According to the law as current in Benares, in default of the son, and son's son and grandson, the widow (supposing the husband's estate to have been distinct and separate) succeeds to the property under the limited tenure

* *Jagannátha* so far differs from the series here given, that he assigns a place next to the maternal uncle's grandson to the maternal great-grandfather and the maternal great-great-grandfather and their descendants. He also is of opinion, that of the male descendants of the paternal grandfather and great-grandfather, those related by the whole blood should exclude those of the half blood.

† See the opinion of Mr. Colebrooke, cited in Elem. Hin. Law, App. 261.

above specified. But if her husband's estate was joint, and held in coparcenary, she is only entitled to maintenance.

In default of the widow, the maiden daughter inherits. In her default, the married indigent daughter. In her default, the married wealthy daughter. Then the daughter's son, but the *Vivádachandra*, the *Vivádaratnakara* and *Vivádachintámani*, authorities which are current in Mithilá, do not enumerate the daughter's son among the series of heirs.* The mother ranks next in the order of succession,† and after her the father. In default of him, brothers of the whole blood succeed; and in their default, those of the half blood.‡

* According to the commentary of *Bálambhatta*, the daughter's daughter inherits, in default of the daughter's son; but this is not the received opinion: and in a case decided by the court of Sadr Diwání Adálat according to the law of Bengal (Sadr Diwání Adálat Reports, vol. ii., p. 290), it was determined, where two of four daughters died during the lifetime of their mother, and one of them left a daughter, which daughter sued her aunts for a fourth of the property in right of her mother, that there was no legal foundation for the claim.

† The same commentator says, the father should inherit first, and then the mother. *Nanda Pandita*, the author of a commentary on the *Mitákshará*, concurs in the opinion of *Bálambhatta. Aparárka* another commentator, *Kamalákara*, the author of the *Vivádatándava*, the authors of the *Smritichandriká*, *Madana Ratna*, *Vyavahúramayú'kha*, *Vivadachandriká*, *Ratnákara*, and other authorities current in Benares, give the father the preference over the mother, and *Jimútavúhana*, *Roghunandana*, and all other Bengal authorities adopt this doctrine; but all the other Benares authorities follow the text of the *Mitákshará*, which assigns the preference to the mother, while *Srikara* maintains that the father and mother inherit together.

‡ *Bálambhatta* is of opinion, that brothers and sisters should inherit together; but this doctrine is not received.

In their default, their sons inherit successively;* then the paternal grandmother;† next the paternal grandfather; the paternal uncle of the whole blood; of the half blood; their sons successively; the paternal great grandmother;‡ the paternal great-grandfather, his son and grandson successively; the paternal great-grandfather's mother;§ his father, his brother, his brother's son. In default of all these, the *Sapindas* in the same order as far as the seventh in degree, which includes only one grade higher in the order of ascent than the heirs above enumerated. In default of *Sapindas,* the *Samánodakas* succeed: and these include the above enumerated heirs in the same order as far as the fourteenth in degree.|| In default of the *Samánodakas,* the *Bundhús* or cognates succeed. These kindred are of three descriptions; personal, paternal, and maternal. The personal kindred are, the sons of his own father's sister, the sons of his own mother's sister, and the sons of his own maternal uncle. The paternal kindred are, the sons of his father's paternal aunt, the sons of his father's maternal aunt, and the sons of his father's maternal

* And, according to *Bálambhatta,* brothers' daughters, and brothers' sons inherit together; but neither is this opinion followed.

† *Srikara Acharya* maintains that the brother's grandsons have a title to the succession in default of the brothers' sons; and this opinion is also held by the author of the *Vivádachandriká,* but by no other authority; and there is the same difference of opinion, as to the relative priority of the grandmother, as has been noticed in the case of the father and mother.

‡ The same difference of opinion exists in this case also.

§ And in this case.

|| The term *Gotraja* (or gentiles) has been defined to signify *Sapindas* and *Samánodakas* by *Bálambhatta* and in the *Subodhini,* etc.

uncle. His maternal kindred are, the sons of his mother's paternal aunt, the sons of his mother's maternal aunt, and the sons of his mother's maternal uncle.* In default of them, the *Acharya* or spiritual preceptor; the pupil, fellow student in theology, learned Brahmins; and lastly, always excepting the property of Brahmins, the estate escheats to the ruling power.

The order of succession as it obtains in Mithilá corresponds with what is here laid down. In the case of Gangadatt Iha *v.* Srínarayan and Musst. Lílavatí (Sadr Diwání Adálat Reports, vol. ii. p. 11), it was determined, that according to the law as current in Mithilá, claimants to inheritance, as far as the seventh (*Sapindas*) and even the fourteenth in descent (*Samánodakas*) in the male line from a common ancestor, are preferable to the cousin by the mother's side of the deceased proprietor; that is to say, his mother's sister's son. Had the case in question been decided according to the law of Bengal (which, the parties there residing, would have so happened, had it not been determined that a person settling in a foreign district shall not be deprived of the laws of his native district, provided he adhere to its customs and usages) the mother's sister's son would have obtained the preference; that individual ranking, agreeably to the law of Bengal, between the

* See *Mitákshará*, p. 352. In this series, no provision appears to have been made for the maternal relations in the ascending line; but *Vachespatimisra* in the *Vivádachintámani*, assigns to "the maternal uncle and the rest" (*Matúladi*), a place in the order of succession next to the *Samánodakas*; and *Mitramisra*, in the *Víramitrodaya*, expresses his opinion, that, as the maternal uncle's son inherits, he himself should be held to have the same right by analogy.

Sapindas and the *Samánodakas*, as was exemplified in the case of Rúscharau Mohapater *v.* Anand Lal Khan (Sadr Diwání Adálat Reports, vol. ii. p. 35), in which it was determined, according to an exposition of the Hindu law as current in Bengal, that the son of a maternal uncle (who is also a Bandhu) takes the inheritance in preference to lineal descendants from a common ancestor, beyond the third in ascent.

The order of succession, agreeably to the law as current in the south of India, does not appear to differ from that of Benares.

In the Vyavaháramayūk'ha, an authority of great eminence in the west of India, a considerable deviation from the above order appears; and the heirs, after the mother, are thus enumerated. The brother of the whole blood, his son, the paternal grandmother, the sister,* the paternal grandfather, and the brother of the half blood, who inherit together. In default of these the *Sapindas*, the *Samánodakas*, and the *Bandhús* inherit successively, according to their degree of proximity.

It may be stated, as a general principle of the law as applicable to all schools, that he with whom rests the right of performing obsequies is entitled to preference in the order of succession; but there are exceptions to this rule;

* The Bombay Reports, vol. ii., 471, exhibit a case demonstrative of the sister's right according to this doctrine, and in a suit between two cousins for the property of their maternal uncle, it was held that neither had any right during the lifetime of their uncle's sister. There is another similar case in vol. i., p. 71. But this admission of the sister seems peculiar to the doctrine followed on that side of India. See Colebrooke, cited in Appendix, Elem. Hin. Law, p. 252.

for instance, in the case of a widow dying and leaving a brother and daughter her surviving, the daughter takes to the exclusion of the brother, although the exequial ceremonies must be performed by the latter.* The passages of Hindu law which intimate that the succession to the estate and the right of performing obsequies go together, do not imply that the mere act of celebrating the funeral rites gives a title to the succession; but that the successor is bound to the due performance of the last rites for the person whose wealth has devolved on him.†

* Elem. Hin. Law, App., p. 245 and 251.

† Note to S. D. A. Reports, vol. i., p. 22.

CHAPTER III.

OF STRIDHAN, OR WOMAN'S SEPARATE PROPERTY.

This description of property is not governed by the ordinary rules of inheritance. It is peculiar and distinct, and the succession to it varies according to circumstances. It varies according to the condition of the woman, and the means by which she became possessed of the property.*

* According to the Hindu Law, there are several sorts of this species of property, some of which are as follows. *Adhyágnika*, or what was given before the nuptial fire. *Adhyáváhana*, or what was given at the bridal procession. *Prítidatta*, or what was given in token of affection. *Mátri pitri* and *bhrátridatta*, or what was received from a mother, father, and brother. *Adhividánika*, or a gift on a second marriage, *i.e.*, wealth given by a man for the sake of satisfying his first wife, when desirous of espousing a second. *Paranayanam*, or *paraphernalia*. *Anwadhayika*, or gift subsequent. *Sandayika*, or gift from affectionate kindred. *Sulka*, or perquisite. (It is more usually understood to mean dower or property settled on the bride. W.) *Yautuka*, or what was received at marriage. *Pádabandánika*, or what was given to the wife in return of her humble salutation. Some lawyers class the *Prítidatta* and the *Pádabandánika* as one species of woman's property, under the appellation of *Lávanyárjita*, or what was gained by loveliness.

In the *Mitákshará*, whatever a woman may have acquired, whether by inheritance, purchase, partition, seizure, or finding, is denominated woman's property, but it does not constitute her *peculium*. Authors differ in their enumeration of the various sorts of *Stridhan*, some confining the number to eight, others to six, others to five, and others to three; but as the difference consists in a more or less comprehensive classification, it does not require any particular notice. The most comprehensive definition of a married woman's *peculium* is given in the following text of *Manu*:—"What was given before the nuptial fire, what was given at the bridal procession, what was given in token of love, and what was received from a mother, a brother, or a father, are considered as the sixfold separate property of a married woman."* And it may be here observed that *Stridhan* which has once devolved according to the law of succession which governs the descent of this peculiar species of property, ceases to be ranked as such, and is ever afterwards governed by the ordinary rules of inheritance: for instance, property given to a woman on her marriage is *Stridhan*, and passes to her daughter at her death; but at the daughter's death it passes to the heir of the daughter like other property; and the brother of her mother would be heir in preference to her own daughter, such daughter being a widow without issue.

To such property left by an unmarried woman, the heirs are her brother, her father, and her mother suc-

* § 365.

cessively; and failing these, her paternal kinsmen in due order.

To such property left by a married woman given to her at the time of her nuptials, the heirs are her daughters; the maiden, as in the ordinary law of inheritance, ranking first, and then the married daughter likely to have male issue.* The barren and the widowed daughters, failing the two first, succeed as coheirs. In default of daughters, the son succeeds; then the daughter's son,† the son's son, the great-grandson in the male line, the son of a contemporary wife, her grandson and her great-grandson in the male line. In default of all these descendants, supposing the marriage to have been celebrated according to any of the first five forms,‡ the husband succeeds, and the brother, the mother, the father. But if celebrated according to any of the three last forms,§ the brother is preferred to the husband, and both are postponed to the mother and father.

* It may here be mentioned, that at the death of a maiden or betrothed daughter on whom the inheritance had devolved, and who proved barren, or on the death of a widow who had not given birth to a son, the succession of the property which they had so inherited, will devolve next on the sisters having and likely to have male issue; and in their default, on the barren and widowed daughters.

† According to *Jimūtavdhana*, the right of the daughter's son is postponed to that of the son of the contemporary wife; but his opinion in this respect is refuted by *Srikrishna* and other eminent authorities.

‡ For an enumeration of these forms, see the chapter of *Manu* on Marriage.

§ The justice of this order of succession does not at first sight seem obvious, at least as regards the *Asura* marriage, where money is advanced by the family of the bridegroom, and to which, therefore, it would appear equitable that it should revert on the death of the bride.

In default of these, the heirs are successively as follows:—Husband's younger brother, his younger brother's son, his elder brother's son, the sister's son, husband's sister's son, the brother's son, the son-in-law, the father-in-law, the elder brother-in-law, the *Sapindas*, the *Sakulyas*, the *Samánodakas*.

To such property left by a married woman given to her by her father, but not at the time of her nuptials, the heirs are successively, a maiden daughter, a son, a daughter who has or is likely to have male issue, daughter's son, son's son, son's grandson, the great-grandson in the male line, the son of a contemporary wife, her grandson, her great-grandson in the male line. In default of all these, the barren and the widowed daughters succeed as coheirs, and then the succession goes as in the five first forms of marriage.

To such property left by a married woman not given to her by her father, and not given to her at the time of her nuptials, the heirs are in the same order as above, with the exception that the son and unmarried daughter inherit together, and not successively, and that the son's son is preferred to the daughter's son.*

It may here be observed, that the Hindu law recognizes the absolute dominion of a married woman over

* But *Raghunandana* holds, that in the case of a married woman dying without issue, the husband alone has a right to the property of his wife, bestowed on her by him after marriage; but that the brother has in such case the prior right to any property which may have been given to her by her father and mother.

her separate and peculiar property, except land given to her by her husband, of which she is at liberty to make any disposition at pleasure. The husband has nevertheless power to use the woman's *peculium*, and consume it in case of distress; and she is subject to his control, even in regard to her separate and peculiar property.*

* The order above given is chiefly taken from Colebrooke's translation of the *Dáyabhága*, p. 100. I do not find that the law in this particular varies materially in the different schools; except that (as in the case of succession to ordinary property) a distinction is made by the law of Benares and other schools, between wealthy and indigent daughters. There are also many other nice distinctions and discrepancies of opinion, of which the following are specimens, and which it is unimportant to notice at greater length in this place. According to *Jímútaváhana* and the mass of Bengal authorities, the property of a deceased woman not received at her nuptials and not given to her by her father, goes to her son and to her unmarried daughters in equal portions, whether the latter have been betrothed or otherwise. *Jagannátha* is of opinion, that the succession of a daughter who has been betrothed is barred by the claim of one who has not been affianced, and that both cannot have an equal right to inherit with a brother. *Raghunandana* denies that there is any text justifying the succession of a betrothed daughter. The authors of the *Vyavahára mayúk'ha*, and *Víramitrodaya* distinctly state, that in default of a maiden daughter, a married one whose husband is living takes the inheritance with her brother. According to the *Mitákshará* and other ancient authorities current in Benares, the brothers and sisters cannot under any circumstances inherit together; while *Madhaváchárya* states, that sons and daughters inherit their mother's *peculium* together, only where it was derived from the family of the husband, and *Vachaspati Bhattáchárya*, on the other hand, contends they inherit simultaneously in every instance, excepting that of property received at nuptials, and given by parents. The conflicting doctrines in matters such as the above, of minor moment, might be multiplied almost *ad infinitum*.

CHAPTER IV.

OF PARTITION.

HAVING treated of the subject of property acquired by succession, it remains to treat of that which is acquired by partition while the ancestor survives, and by partition among the heirs, after succession.

The father's consent is requisite to partition, and while he lives, the sons have not, according to the law of Bengal, the power to exact it, except under such circumstances as would altogether divest him of his proprietary right, such as his degradation, or his adoption of a religious life.

Jagannátha has, indeed, expressed an opinion, that sons, oppressed by a step-mother or the like, may apply to the king, and obtain a partition from their father of the patrimony inherited from the grandfather, though not a partition of the wealth acquired by the father himself. To the father's right of making a partition there is but one condition annexed, namely, that the mother be past child-bearing, and this condition applies to ancestral immoveable property alone: as to his self-acquired estate, whether it consist of moveable or immoveable property, and the ancestral property of whatever description which may have been usurped by a stranger, but recovered by the father, his own consent is the only requisite to partition. But the law as current in Benares and other schools, differs widely from that of Bengal, in respect to partition of the ancestral estate, which according to the former may be enforced at the pleasure of the sons, if the mother be incapable of bearing more issue, even though the father retain his worldly affections, and though he be averse to partition.*

According to the law of Bengal, the father may make an unequal distribution of property acquired by himself exclusively, as well as of moveable ancestral property, and of property of whatever description recovered by himself, retaining in his own hands as much as he may think fit; and should the distribution he makes be unequal, or should he without just cause exclude any one of his sons, the act is valid though sinful: not so with respect to the ancestral immoveable property and estate, to the acquisition of which his sons may have contributed: of such property the sons are entitled to equal shares; but the father may retain a double share of it, as well as of acquisitions made by his sons.

The law of Benares, on the other hand, prohibits any unequal distribution by the father of ancestral property of whatever description, as well as of immoveable property acquired by himself. At a distribution of his own personal acquisitions even, he cannot,

* *Miták.*, ch. i., sec. 2, § 7.

according to the same law, reserve more than two shares for himself; and as the maxim of *factum valet* does not apply in that school, any unequal distribution of real property must be considered as not only sinful, but illegal.*

This subject has been treated of at great length by the author of the Considerations on Hindu Law, in the chapter on gifts and unequal distribution: and though he confesses it to be one of a most perplexing nature, from the variety of opposite decisions to which it has given rise, yet he inclines to the opinion, that a gift of even the entire ancestral and immoveable property to one son, to the exclusion of the rest, is sinful, but nevertheless *valid,* if made. It must be recollected, that he was treating of the law as current in Bengal only, and not elsewhere. My reasons for arriving at an opposite opinion are; first, because the doctrine for which I contend has been established by the latest decision, founded on a more minute and deliberate investigation of the law of the case than had ever before been made; and secondly, because the only authority for the reverse of this doctrine consists in the following passages from the *Dáyabhága*:—"The texts of *Vyása* exhibiting a prohibition are intended to show a moral offence; they are not meant to invalidate the sale or other transfer. Therefore, since it is denied

* Though as the father is not precluded from disposing of moveables at his discretion, a *gift* of such property to one son should be deemed valid. Colebrooke, cited in Elem. Hin. Law, App. p. 5; and as to the father's incompetency to dispose of immoveable property, though acquired by himself, see Ibid., p. 7.

that a gift or sale should be made, the precept is infringed by making one; but the gift or transfer is not null, for a fact cannot be altered by a hundred texts." Now if these passages are to be taken in a general sense; if they are to be held to have the effect of legalising or at least rendering valid all acts committed in direct opposition to the law, they must have the effect of superseding all law; and it would be better at once to pronounce those texts alone to be the guide for our judicial decisions. The example adduced by the commentator to illustrate these texts, clearly shows the spirit in which this unmeaning, though mischievous dogma was delivered; he declares that a fact cannot be altered by a hundred texts, in the same manner as the murder of a Brahmin, though in the highest degree criminal and unlawful, having been perpetrated, there is no remedy, or in other words, that the defunct Brahmin cannot be brought to life again. The illustration might be apposite, if there were no such thing as retribution, and if the law did not exact all possible amends for the injury inflicted. But what renders this conclusion less disputable is, that the texts of *Vyása* in question occur in the chapter of the *Dáyabhága* which treats of self-acquisitions, and has no reference to ancestral property. If any additional proof be wanting of the father's incompetency to dispose of ancestral real property by an unequal partition, or to do any other act with it which might be prejudicial to the interests of his son, I would merely refer to the provision contained in the translation of the extract from the Mitákshará relative to judicial proceedings. The rule is in the following terms: "The ownership of the father and son is the same in land which was acquired by his father," etc. From this text it appears, that in the case of land acquired by the grandfather, the ownership of father and son is equal; and therefore if the father make away with the immoveable property so acquired by the grandfather, and if the son has recourse to a court of justice, a judicial proceeding will be entertained between the father and son. The passage occurs in a dissertation as to who are fit parties in judicial proceeding; and although the indecorum of a contest wherein the father and son are litigant parties has been expressly recognized, yet, at the same time, the rights of the son are declared to be of so inviolable a nature, that an action by him for the maintenance of them will lie against his father, and that it is better there should be a breach of moral decorum than a violation of legal right.

The question as to the extent to which an unequal distribution made by a father in the province of Bengal should be upheld, has been amply discussed also in the report of a case decided by the court of Sadr Diwání Adálat, in the year 1816,* wherein it was determined, that an unequal distribution of ancestral immoveable property is illegal and invalid, and that the

* For the whole of the argument, see Sadr Diwání Adálat Reports, vol. ii., p. 214.

unequal distribution of property acquired by the father, and of moveable ancestral property, is legal and valid, unless when made under the influence of a motive which is held in law to deprive a person of the power to make a distribution. It was declared, in a note to that case, that the validity of an unequal distribution of ancestral immoveable property, such as is expressly forbidden by the received authorities on Hindu law, cannot be maintained on any construction of that law, by *Jimûtaváhana* and others. *Jagannátha,* in his Digest, maintains an opinion opposite to this, and lays it down, that if a father, infringing the law, absolutely give away the whole or part of the immoveable ancestral property, such gift is valid, provided he be not under the influence of anger or other disqualifying motive: and admitting this doctrine to be correct, it must be inferred *à fortiori* that he is authorized to make an unequal distribution of such property, but the reverse of this doctrine has been established by the mass of authorities cited in the case above alluded to.

In the event of a son being born after partition made by the father, he will be sole heir to the property retained by the father; and if none have been retained, the other sons are bound to contribute to a share out of their portions. According to *Jimûtaváhana, Raghunandana, Srikrishna,* and other Bengal authors, when partition is made by a father, a share equal to that of a son must be given to the childless wife, not to her who has male issue. But the doctrine laid down by Harináthá is, that if the father reserve two or more shares, no share need be assigned to the wives, because their maintenance may be supplied out of the portion reserved. It is also laid down in the *Vivádárnavesetu,* that an equal share to a wife is ordained, in a case where the father gives equal shares to his sons; but that where he gives unequal portions, and reserves a larger share for himself, he is bound to allot to each of his wives, from the property reserved by himself, as much as may amount to the average share of a son. These shares to wives are allotted only in case of no property having been given to them. According to some authorities, if a wife had received property elsewhere, a moiety of a son's share should be allotted to her; but according to other authorities the difference should be made up to the wives between what they have received and a son's share. The doctrine maintained by *Jagannátha* is, that if the wife has received, from any quarter, wealth which would ultimately have devolved on her husband, such wealth should be included in the calculation of her allotment; but if she received the property from her own father or other relative, or from the maternal uncle or other collateral kinsman of her husband, it should not be included, her husband not having any interest therein.

The law as current in Benares, Mithilá, and elsewhere, differs from the Bengal school on this subject, and is not in itself uniform or consistent. *Vijnyáneswara* ordains: "When the father, by his own choice, makes all his sons partakers of equal portions, his wives, to whom peculiar property had not been given by their husband or father-in-law, must be made participants of shares equal to those of sons."

But if separate property had been given, the same authority subsequently directs the allotment of half a share; "or if any had been given, let him assign a half." According to *Mádhavácharjya*, if the father by his own free will make his sons equal participants, he ought to make his wives, to whom no separate property has been given, partakers of a share equal to that of a son; but if such property has been presented to her, then a moiety should be given. *Kamalákára* the author of the *Vivádatándava*, declares generally, that whether the father be living or dead, his wives are respectively entitled to a son's portion. But *Sulapáni*, in the *Dipakálika*, maintains, that if the father make an equal partition among his sons by his own choice, he must give equal shares to such of his wives only as have no male issue: and *Halayudha* also lays it down, that wives who have no sons are here intended. *Misra* contends, that "when he reserves the greater part of his fortune, and gives some trifle to his sons, or takes a double share for himself, the husband must give so much wealth to his wives out of his own share alone: accordingly the separate delivery of shares to wives is only ordained when he makes an equal partition." The sum of the above arguments seems to be, that in the case of an equal partition made by a father among his sons, his wives who are destitute of male issue take equal portions; that, where he reserves a large portion for himself, his wives are not entitled to any specific share, but must be maintained by him; and that, where unequal shares are given to sons, the average of the shares of the sons should be taken for the purpose of ascertaining the allotments of the wives. The same rules apply also to paternal grandmothers, in case of partition of the ancestral property.

At any time after the death, natural or civil, of their parents, the brethren are competent to come to a partition among themselves of the property, moveable and immoveable, ancestral and acquired; and, according to the law as received in the province of Bengal, the widow is not only entitled to share an undivided estate with the brethren of her husband, but she may require from them a partition of it, although her allotment will devolve on the heirs of her husband at her decease.* Partition may be made also while the mother survives. This rule, though at variance with the doctrine of *Jimútaváhana* has nevertheless been maintained by more modern authorities, and is universally observed in practice.†

Nephews whose fathers are dead, are entitled, as far as the fourth in descent, to participate equally with the brethren. These take *per stirpes*, and any one of the coparceners may insist on the partition of his share.‡

* See note to the case of Bhyróchand Rai, *v.* Rassikmaní, Sadr Diwáni Adálat Reports, vol. i., p. 28, and case of Nílkant Rai, *v.* Maní Chowdrain; ibid., 58; also case of Ráni Bhawáni Dibia and another, *v.* Raní Súrajmaní, ibid., p. 135. The reverse is the case, according to the law of Benares. See the case of Daljít Singh, *v.* Shermanik Singh, ibid. 59.

† Dig. vol. iii., 78.

‡ *Katyáyana*, cited in Dig. vol. iii., 7; and see Elem. Hin. Law, App. 292.

But in all such cases, to each of the father's wives who is a mother, must be assigned a share equal to that of a son, and to the childless wives a sufficient maintenance; but according to the *Mitákshará* and other works current in Benares and the southern provinces, childless wives are also entitled to shares, the term *mata* being interpreted to signify both mother and step-mother. The *Smritichandriká* is the only authority which altogether excludes a mother from the right of participation. To the unmarried daughters such portions are allotted as may suffice for the due celebration of their nuptials.* This portion has been fixed at the fourth of the share of a brother: in other words, supposing there is one son and one daughter, the estate should be made into two parts, and one of those two parts made into four. The daughter takes one of these fourths. If there be two sons and one daughter, the estate should be made into three parts, and one of these three parts made into four. The daughter takes one of these fourths, or a twelfth. If there be one son and two daughters, the estate should be made into three parts, and two of those three parts made into four. The daughters each take one of these fourths.† But according to the best authorities, these proportions are not universally assignable; for where the estate is either too small to admit of this being given without inconvenience, or too large to render the gift of such portion unnecessary to the due celebration of the nuptials, the

* Elem. Hin. Law, App. 86 and 97.

† *Miták.* On Inheritance, chap. i., § 7.

sisters are entitled to so much only as may suffice to defray the expenses of the marriage ceremony. In fine, this provision for the sisters, intended to uphold the general respectability of the family, is accorded rather as a matter of indulgence, than prescribed as a matter of right.*

Any improvement of joint property effected by one of the brethren, does not confer on him a title to a greater share;† but an acquisition made by one, by means of his own unassisted and exclusive labour, entitles the acquirer, according to the law as current in Bengal, to a double share on partition. And it was ruled by the Sadr Diwání Adálat, that where an estate is acquired by one of four brothers living together, either with aid from joint funds, or with personal aid from the brothers, two fifths should be given to the acquirer, and one fifth to each of the other three.‡ But according to the law as current in Benares, the fact of one brother having contributed personal labour while no exertion was made by the other, is not a ground of distinction. If the patrimonial stock was used, all the brethren share alike.§ If the joint stock have not been

* The question has been fully discussed by the author of the Considerations on Hindu Law, p. 103 et seq. The inconsistency of the rules has been pointed out; but the same conclusion is arrived at, namely, that the sister's is a claim rather than a right. See the opinion of Mr. Sutherland cited in Elem. Hin. Law, App. p. 301, which is to the same effect, and of Mr. Colebrooke, ibid., p. 361 and 385.

† *Miták.* Chap. i., sec. 3, § 4; and Precedents, Case 15, vol. ii. Chap. Effects liable and not liable to partition (note).

‡ S. D. A. Rep., vol. i., p. 6.

§ See note to Precedents, Case 4. Chap. Of Sons, etc., vol. ii.

used,* he by whose sole labour the acquisition has been made is alone entitled to the benefit of it.† And where property has been acquired without aid from joint funds, by the exclusive industry of one member of an undivided family, others of the same family, although they were at the time living in coparcenary with him, have no right to participate in his acquisition.‡ The rule is the same with respect to property recovered, excepting land, of which the party recovering it is entitled to a fourth more than the rest of his brethren.§ It has also been ruled, that if lands are acquired partly by the labour of one brother, and partly by the capital of another, each is entitled to half a share; and that if they were acquired by the joint labour and capital of one, and by the labour only of the other, two thirds should belong to the former, and one third to the latter; but this provision seems rather to be founded on a principle of equity, than any specific rule of Hindu law.‖

Presents received at nuptials, as well as the acquisitions of learning and valour, are, generally speaking, not claimable by the brethren on partition: but for a more detailed account of indivisible and specially partible, the reader is referred to the translation of *Jagannátha's*

* What constitutes the use of joint stock is not unfrequently very difficult to determine, and no general rule can be laid down applicable to all cases that may arise. Each individual case must be decided on its own merits. See Elem. Hin. Law, App. p. 306.

† Dig. vol. iii., 110.

‡ Kalípershaud Rai and others, *v.* Digumber Rai and others, Precedents, vol. ii., p. 237.

§ *Sankha*, cited in ibid., 365; and Elem. Hin. Law, App. p. 313.

‖ Case of Koshul Chakrawatí, *v.* Radhánath, S. D. A. Reports, vol. i., p. 336.

Digest, vol. iii., p. 332 et seq., and to the chapter in vol. ii. treating of effects liable and not liable to partition. According to the more correct opinion, where there is an undivided residue, it is not subject to the ordinary rules of partition of joint property: in other words, if at a general partition any part of the property was left joint, the widow of a deceased brother will not participate, notwithstanding the separation, but such undivided residue will go exclusively to the brother.*

Partition may be made without having recourse to writing or other formality; and in the event of its being disputed at any subsequent period, the fact may be ascertained by circumstantial evidence. It cannot always be inferred from the manner in which the brethren live, as they may reside apparently in a state of union, and yet, in matters of property, each may be separate; while, on the other hand, they may reside apart and yet may be in a state of union with respect to property: though it undoubtedly is one among the presumptive proofs to which recourse may be had, in a case of uncertainty, to determine whether a family be united or separate in regard to acquisitions and property.† The only criterion seems to consist in their entering into distinct contracts, in their becoming sureties one for the other, or in their separate performance of other similar acts, which tend to show, that they have no dependence on or connexion with each other.‡ In

* Elem. Hin. Law, App. p. 322.

† See note to Sadr Diwání Adálat Reports, vol. i., p. 36.

‡ Dig. vol. iii., 414; and see Cases, Chap. of Evidence of Partition; also Colebrooke, cited in App. Elem. Hin. Law, p. 325 et seq.

case of an undivided Hindu family, the court of Sadr Diwání Adálat were of opinion that their acquisitions should be presumed to have been joint till proved otherwise, the *onus probandi* resting with the party claiming exclusive right;* and, in another case, a member of a Hindu family, among whom there had been no formal articles of separation, but who, as well as his father, messed separately from the rest, and had no share of their profits and loss in trade, though he had occasionally been employed by them, and had received supplies for his private expenses, was presumed to be separate, and not allowed a share of the acquisition made by others of the family.† The law is particularly careful of the rights of those who may be born subsequent to a partition made by the father. With respect to ancestral property, it is not likely that the just claims of any heirs can be defeated, as the law prohibits partition so long as the mother is capable of bearing issue; but to guard against the possibility of such an occurrence it is provided, that the father shall retain two shares, to which shares, if a son be subsequently born, he is exclusively entitled. There is another provision also which forms an effectual safeguard against the destitution of children born subsequently to a partition, which consists in the father's right of resumption, in case of necessity, of the property which he may have distributed among his sons.‡

* Case of Gourchandra Rai and others, *v.* Harichandra Rai and others, S. D. A. Reports, vol. iv., p. 162.

† Rajkishor Rai and others, *v.* the widow of Santú Das, S. D. A. Reports, vol. i., 13.

‡ See Precedents, Case 3. Chap. of Partition, vol. ii.

CHAPTER V.

OF MARRIAGE.

On the subject of marriage, it may be presumed that it has not often constituted a matter of litigation in the civil courts, from the circumstance, that points connected with it do not appear to have been referred to the Hindu law officers. Disputes connected with this topic, as well as those relating to matters of caste generally, are, for the most part, adjusted by reference to private arbitration. It is otherwise in the provinces subject to the presidencies of Madras and Bombay, where many matrimonial disagreements and questions relative to caste have been submitted to the adjudication of the established European court.* As, however, questions relative to marriage are among those which the Company's courts are, by law, called upon to decide, it may not be amiss to cite some of the fundamental rules connected with the institution.

* See Appendix Elem. Hin. Law, p. 22 et passim, and Bombay Reports, p. 11, 35, 363, 370, 379, and 389, vol. i., and p. 108, 323, 434, 473, 576 and 685, vol. ii.

Marriage among the Hindus is not merely a civil contract, but a sacrament; forming the last of the ceremonies prescribed to the three regenerate classes, and the only one for *Sudras*;* and an unmarried man has been declared to be incapacitated for the performance of religious duties.† It is well known that women are betrothed at a very early period of life, and it is this betrothment, in fact, which constitutes marriage. The contract is then valid and binding to all intents and purposes. It is complete and irrevocable immediately on the performance of certain ceremonies,‡ without consummation. Second marriages, after the death of the husband first espoused, are wholly unknown to the Hindu law;§ though in practice, among the inferior castes, nothing is so common. Polygamy is also legally prohibited to men unless for some good and sufficient cause, such as is expressly declared a just ground for dissolving the former contract, as barrenness, disease and the like. This precept, however, is not much adhered to in practice. The text of *Manu*, which in fact prohibits polygamy, has been held, according to modern practice, to justify it. "For the first marriage of the twice-born classes," says *Manu*, "a woman of the same class is recommended;

* Digest, vol. iii., p. 104.

† Ibid., ii., p. 400.

‡ Digest, vol. ii., p. 484; and for an account of ceremonies observed at a marriage, see As. Res., vol. vii., p. 288; also Ward on the Hindus, vol. i., p. 130 et seq.

§ But a widow who, from a wish to bear children, slights her deceased husband *by marrying again*, brings disgrace on herself here below, and shall be excluded from the seat of her lord.—*Manu*, cited in Dig. p. 463, vol. ii.

The Government of India removed by Act xv., of 1856, all legal obstacle to the marriage of Hindu widows. W.

but for such as are impelled by inclination to marry again, women in the direct order of the classes are to be preferred.* From this text it is argued by the moderns, that, as marriage with any woman of a different class is prohibited in the present age, it necessarily follows that a plurality of wives of the same class is admissible; but the inference appears by no means clear, and the practice is admitted by the *pandits* to be reprehensible; though nothing is more common, especially among the *Kúlin*, or highest caste of Brahmins in Bengal.

In the event of a man forsaking his wife without just cause, and marrying another, he shall pay his first wife a sum equal to the expenses of his second marriage, provided she have not received any *Stridhan*, or make it up to her, if she have; but he is not required in any case, to assign more than a third of his property. In all cases, and for whatever cause a wife may have been deserted, she is entitled to sufficient maintenance. In the *Mitákshará*, a distinction is made. Where a second wife is married, there being a legal objection to the first, she is entitled to a sum equal to the expenses incurred in the second marriage; but where no objection whatever exists to the first wife, a third of the husband's property should be given as a compensation.† But in modern practice, a husband considers it quite sufficient to maintain a superseded wife, by providing her with food and raiment.

* *Manu*, chap. iii., § 12.

† *Yajnyawalkya*, cited in Dig. vol. ii., p. 420; and see a case stated, Elem. Hin. Law, App. p. 51.

There are eight forms of marriage: The *Bráhma, Daiva, Ársha, Prájapatya, Ásura, Gándharva, Rákshasa,* and *Paisácha.*

The four first forms are peculiar to the *Brahminical* tribe. The principle in these contracts seems to be, that the parties are mutually consenting, and actuated by disinterested motives.

The fifth form is peculiar to *Vaisyas* and *Sudras.* It is reprobated, on the principle of its being a mercenary contract, consented to by the father of the girl for a pecuniary consideration. The sixth and seventh forms are peculiar to the military tribe, where the union is founded either on reciprocal affection or the right of conquest. And the eight or last is reprobated for all, being accomplished by means of fraud and circumvention.*

The most usual form of marriage is that of the *Bráhma,* which is completed "when the damsel is given by her father, when he has decked her, as elegantly as he can, to the bridegroom whom he has invited," the nuptials of course being celebrated with the usual ceremonies. The next species of marriage most usually practised is that of the *Ásura,* where a pecuniary consideration is received by the father; and I am given to understand that marriages by the *Paisácha* mode are not uncommon; and that young women, who from their wealth or beauty may be desirable objects, are not unfrequently inveigled by artifice into matrimony; the forms of which once gone through, the contract

* Digest, vol. iii., p. 606.

is not dissoluble on any plea of fraud, or even of force.*

The *Gándharva* marriage is the only one of the eight modes for the legalizing of which no forms are necessary;† and it seems that mutual cohabitation, as it implies what the law declares to be alone necessary, namely, "reciprocal amorous agreement," would be sufficient to establish such a marriage if corroborated by any word or deed on the part of the man.‡

The relations with whom it is prohibited to contract matrimony are thus enumerated by *Manu:* "She who is not descended from his *paternal* or *maternal* ancestors within the sixth degree, and who is not *known by her family name to be* of the same primitive stock with his

* This is not the only instance in which fraud is legalized by the Hindu law. That law sets aside gifts or promises made for the purpose of delusion, though this is fraud on the part of the person who practises the imposition, and can entitle him to no relief. The same law allows to the creditor a lien upon a deposit or commodate in his hands for the recovery of his due from the debtor who so entrusts any article to him; and even permits the practice of trick and artifice, to obtain possession of such an article with the purpose of retaining it as a pledge.—Colebrooke, Obl. and Con., Book ii., § 95, and Book iv., § 518.

It may be doubted if such cases occur. Hindu girls are betrothed as children, and their consent has nothing to do with the engagement which is binding. W.

† This form of marriage is declared to be peculiar to the military tribe. May not the indulgence have originated in principles similar to those by which, according both to the civil and English law, soldiers are permitted to make nuncupative wills, and to dispose of their property without those forms which the law requires in other cases?—Bl. Comm., vol. i., p. 417.

‡ On this principle the law officers of the Sadr Diwání Adálat declared legal a marriage contracted in Cuttack, not very long ago, in a case where the parties had cohabited for some time, and the man signified his intention by placing a garland of flowers round the neck of the woman. See also Elem. Hin. Law, App. p. 198.

father or *mother*, is eligible by a twice-born man for nuptials and holy union."

Adultery is a criminal, but not a civil offence, and an action for damages as preferred by the husband will not lie against the adulterer.* It is not a sufficient cause for the wife to desert the husband, and there are not many predicaments in which such an act on her part is justifiable. Insanity, impotence, and degradation, are, perhaps, the only circumstances under which her desertion of her husband would not be considered as a punishable offence.† A married woman has no power to contract, and any contract entered into by her, will neither be binding on herself nor on her husband, unless the subject of the contract be her own peculiar property, or unless she have been entrusted with the management of her husband's affairs; or unless the contract may have been requisite to her obtaining the necessaries of life.‡

* Colebrooke, cited Elem. Hin. Law, App. p. 33. So also our Regulations, following the Múhammadan law in this particular, treat the offence as a crime against society, and not against the individual, but they require that the husband shall stand forward to prosecute. There is a case cited by the author of the Elem. Hin. Law (App. p. 34), in which the *pandits* ruled, that the adulterer was liable for money expended by the injured husband in contracting a second marriage; but this was considered to be rather an equitable opinion, than founded on any express text of law.

† *Manu*, cited in Digest, vol. ii., p. 412.

‡ Colebrooke, Obl. and Con., Part i., Book ii., §§ 57 and 58.

CHAPTER VI.

OF ADOPTION.

The etymology of the Sanscrit word for a son, *putra*, clearly evinces the necessity by which every Hindu considers himself bound to perpetuate his name. "Since the son (trayáte) delivers his father from the hell named *put*, he was, therefore, called *putra* by Brahma himself."* Again: "A son of any description should be anxiously adopted by one who has no male issue, for the funeral cake, water, and solemn rites, and for the celebrity of his name."† Under this feeling, it was natural to resort to the expedient of adoption. Twelve sorts of sons have accordingly been enumerated by *Manu*. "The son begotten by a man himself *in lawful wedlock;* the son of his wife, begotten in the manner before described; a son given *to him; a son made or adopted;* a son of concealed birth or *whose real father cannot be known;* and a son rejected by his natural parents; are the six kinsmen and heirs. The son of

* Institutes of *Manu*, chap. ix., § 138.

† *Smriti*, quoted in the Ratnakara; or, in the language of Statius, "*Orbitas omni fugienda nisu. Orbitas nullo tumulata fletu.*"

a young woman *unmarried*, the son of a pregnant bride, a son bought, a son by a twice married woman, a son self-given, and a son by a Sudra, are the six kinsmen, but not heirs to collaterals." *

In treating of the miscellaneous customs of Greece, the author of the Antiquities † observes as follows:—"Adopted children were called *παιδεσθεται*, or *εισποιητοι*, and were invested in all the privileges and rights of, and obliged to perform all the duties belonging to such as were begotten by their fathers: and being thus provided for in another family, they ceased to have any claim of inheritance and kindred in the family which they had left, unless they first renounced their adoption, which the laws of Solon allowed them not to do, except they had first begotten children to bear the name of the person who had adopted them, thus providing against the ruin of families, which would have been extinguished by the ruin of those who were adopted to preserve them. If the adopted person died without children, the inheritance could not be aliened from the family into which they were adopted, but returned to the relations of the persons who had adopted them. The Athenians are by some thought to have forbidden any man to marry after he had adopted a son, without leave from the magistrate; and there is an instance in Tzetzes's Chiliads of one Leogoras, who being ill-used by Andocides the orator, who was his adopted son, desired leave to marry. However, it is certain that some men married after they had adopted

* Institutes of *Manu*, chap. ix., §§ 159 and 160.

† Vol. ii., p. 336.

sons; and if they begot legitimate children, their estates were equally shared between those begotten and adopted."

The whole, or nearly the whole, of the provisions above cited, are strictly applicable to the system of adoption as it prevails among the Hindus at this day. But the renunciation of adoption is a thing unheard of in these provinces, and unsanctioned by law under any circumstances. There is no express text declaring illegal a renunciation of adoption, but at the same time there is not any which can be construed as approaching to a justification of it.

In the present age, two, or at the most three, forms of adoption only are allowed, in these provinces; and the *Dattaka*, or son given, and the *Kritrima*, or son made, are the most common. The latter form obtains only in the province of Mithilá. In strictness, perhaps, adoption in this form should be held to be abrogated, as the filiation of any but a son legally begotten, or given in adoption, is declared obsolete in the present age;* but agreeably to a text of *Vrihaspati*, immemorial usage legalizes any practice.† Some of the requisite conditions for the adoption of a son are comprised in the following texts of *Manu*:—"He whom his father, or mother‡ with her husband's assent, gives to another as his son, provided that the donee have no

* See general note by Sir W. Jones, appended to his translation of *Manu's* Institutes; and the text of the *Aditya Purána*, cited in *Jagannátha's* Digest, vol. iii., p. 272.

† Cited in the Digest, vol. ii., p. 128.

‡ Section 4, § 12.

issue, if the boy be of the same class, and affectionately disposed, is considered as a son given, *the gift being confirmed by pouring water.*" "He is considered as a son made *or adopted,* whom a man takes as his own son, the boy being equal in class, endued with filial virtues, acquainted with the merit of *performing obsequies to his adopter,* and with the sin of omitting them."* But there are many conditions besides these fundamental ones: and briefly noticing such of the rules as are indisputable, and universally admitted, I shall discuss those which have admitted of doubt; and endeavour to fix such as are uncertain, by citing the authorities in support of each. Regarding this particular branch of the law, there is not much difference in the doctrine of the several schools; the *Dattakachandriká* and *Dattakamimánsá,* the two chief authorities on the subject, being respected by all. The first text above cited is sufficiently explicit as to the persons who possess the right of giving in adoption; and the only exception that has been propounded by the commentators is contained in the *Dattakamimánsá,* which refers to the gift of her son by a widow during a season of calamity; and it has been made a question of doubt, whether a widow, even with the sanction of her husband expressed before his decease, is competent to adopt a son, but her competency so to do is established by the prevailing authorities. It has been ruled, however, that in the case of an adoption made by a widow without having obtained the consent of her husband (or in which

* Institutes of *Manu,* chap. ix., §§ 168 and 169.

the adopted son shall not have been delivered over to her by either of his parents, but only by his brother) the adoption is invalid.* It is required that the party adopting † should be destitute of a son, and son's son and son's grandson; ‡ that the party adopted should neither be the only nor the eldest son,§ nor an elder

* Case of Taramani Dibia, *v.* Deo Narayan Rai, and another, Sadr Diwání Adálat Reports, vol. iii., p. 387. The same principle was recognized in the case of Raja Shumsher Mall, *v.* Ranee Dilraj Kúnvar, vol. ii., p. 169.

† It has been doubted by Mr. Sutherland, in his Synopsis, whether an unmarried person, that is one not a *grihi*, or as we would say, a bachelor, is competent to adopt; but he inclines to the affirmative of the question (p. 212). In the Precedents, part ii., of this work in the case of adoption No. 1, the *pandits* expressly declared the adoption by such individual to be legal and valid, and there is certainly no authority against it. The same doubt is expressed, and the same conclusion arrived at, with respect to an adoption by a blind, impotent, or lame person.

‡ *Saunaka*, cited in *Datt. Mim.* It has also been doubted by the author of the Considerations (p. 150), whether a man having a grandson by a daughter can adopt a son; but there is no solid foundation on which such a doubt can rest. It must have arisen in the indiscriminate use of the word ("grandson") in the English translations, as applicable to the daughter's son as well as to the son's son. Mr. Sutherland in his Synopsis, p. 212, infers, and justly, that if male issue exist who are disqualified by any legal impediment (such as loss of caste) from the performance of exequial rights, the affiliation of a son may legally take place. In the summary of Hindu Law, p. 48, it is laid down as a rule, that the insanity of a begotten son would not justify adoption by the parent; but to this and other general positions laid down in that work I cannot altogether accede: for instance, it is stated, that the *Púna Shastrís* do not recognize the necessity that adoption should precede marriage; that a younger brother may be adopted by an elder one; that the youngest son of a family cannot be adopted, etc., etc., for none of which can I find authority; though undoubtedly the whole of these positions may be just when applied to that side of India, as founded on the *lex loci*, or immemorial custom.

§ *Vasishta*, *Datt. Nir.* and *Manu*, ibid.; but this is rather an injunction against the giving than receiving an elder or only son in adoption, and the transfer having been once made, it cannot be annulled. This seems but reasonable, considering that the adoption having once been made, the relation, such as the paternal or the maternal uncle;* that he should be of the same tribe as the adopting party;† that he should not be the son of one whom the adopter could not have married, such as his sister's son or daughter's son. This last rule, however, applies only to the three superior classes, and does not extend to Sudras.‡ It is a rule also, that when a woman adopts she should have the consent of her husband; or according to the law laid down in some authorities, the sanction of his kindred;§ that where there is a brother's son, he should be selected for adoption in preference to all other individuals; but this is not universally indispensable, so as to invalidate the adoption of a stranger;‖ *Dattakachandriká*, section 1, § 22. In the case of Uman Datt, pauper, appellant, *v.* Kanhai Singh, it was held, that while a brother's son exists, the adoption of any other individual is illegal; and this is undoubtedly consonant to the doctrine contained in the *Dattakamimánsá*, but it is controverted in the *Dattaka-*

boy *ipso facto* loses all claim to the property of his natural family. See Bombay Reports, case of Haebat Rao, *v.* Govind Rao, vol. ii., p. 75. Also Elem. Hin. Law, App. p. 82, 83.

* *Datt. Mim.* Section 2, § 32. Sadr. Diwání Adálat Reports, vol. iii., p. 232. *Mit.* on Inh. chap. i., sec. ii., p. 12.

† *Manu*, chap. ix., § 168.

‡ *Nareda*, cited in *Datt. Nir.*

§ According to the *Vyavahárakaustubha* and *Mayúk'ha*, authorities of the highest repute among the *Mahrattas*, which in this respect follow the doctrine of the *Dattakachandriká*, the sanction of the husband is not requisite; but in this respect the authorities above cited differ from most others. Bom. Rep., vol. i., p. 181, and vol. ii., p. 76 and 456. See also Elem. Hin. Law, App. p. 66, 68, 71.

‖ Sadr Diwání Adálat Reports, vol. iii., p. 144.

chandriká. It would appear, however, that according to the law of Bengal and elsewhere, where the doctrine of the latter authority is chiefly followed, and where the doctrine of *factum valet* exists, a brother's son may be superseded in favour of a stranger; and even in Benares, and in the places where the *Mimánsá* principally obtains, and where a prohibitory rule has in most instances the effect of law, so as to invalidate an act done in contravention thereto, the adoption of a brother's son or other near relative is not essential, and the validity of an adoption actually made does not rest on the rigid observance of that rule of selection, the choice of him to be adopted being a matter of discretion.* It may be held, then, that the injunction to adopt one's own *Sapinda*, (a brother's son is the first,) and failing them, to adopt one of one's own *Gotra*, is not essential, so as to invalidate the adoption in the event of departure from the rule. It is lastly requisite, that the adopted son should be initiated in the name of the family of the adopting party, with the prescribed form and solemnities.† The adoption being once completed, the son adopted loses all claim to the property of his natural family,‡ but he

* Colebrooke, cited in Elem. Hin. Law, App. p. 74 and 80.

† For an enumeration of the ceremonies enjoined at an adoption, see Summary Hindu Law, p. 52, and Elem. Hin. Law, p. 82, *et seq.;* but the exact observance of these ceremonies is not indispensable. Dig. vol. iii., p. 244, and Elem. Hin. Law, App., pp. 101, 106.

‡ It has been asserted by the author of the Elements of Hindu Law, that a son adopted in the ordinary way, though he cannot marry among his adoptive, yet may one of his natural relations; but I cannot find any authority for this doctrine. He seems to have inferred it from the text of the *Parijata*, "Sons given, purchased, and the rest, who are sons of two fathers, may not marry in either family even: as was the case of

is estranged from his own family only partially. For the purposes of marriage, mourning, etc., he is not considered in the light of a stranger, and the prohibited degrees continue in full force as if he had never been removed. His own family have no claim whatever to any property to which he may have succeeded; and in the event of a son so adopted having succeeded to the property of his adopting father, and leaving no issue, his own father cannot legally claim to inherit from him, but the widow of his adopting father will succeed to the property.* He becomes (with the exception above noticed) to all intents and purposes a member of the family of his adopting father, and he succeeds to his property, collaterally as well as lineally; † but excepting the case of the peculiar adoption termed *Dwyámusháyana*, he is excluded from the participating in his natural father's property. ‡ Where a legitimate son is born subsequently to the adoption, he and the son adopted inherit together; but the adopted son takes one-third, according to the law of Bengal, and one-fourth according to the doctrine of other schools.§ If

Singa and Saisira," that adopted sons not bearing the double relationship might do so; but the inference is clearly untenable. Indeed Mr. Sutherland, to whom he refers as his authority, expressly declares in his Synopsis (p. 219), that the adopted son cannot marry any kinswoman related to his father and mother, within the prohibited degrees, as his consanguineal relation endures.

* Elem. Hin. Law, App., p. 104.

† *Manu*, chap. ix, § 159.

‡ See Precedents of adoption, case 10, and of sister's sons, etc., case 7, *Vasishta*, cited in the *Datt. Mim.* and *Kátyáyana* in the *Dattakachandriká*.

§ See in the case of Srinath Serma *v.* Radhakant, and Datt. Narain Sing and others *v.* Raghubír Singh, Sadr Diwâní Adâlat Reports, vol. i., pp. 15 and 20.

two legitimate sons are subsequently born, then, according to the Benares school, the property should be made into seven parts, of which the legitimate sons would take six; and according to the law as current elsewhere, into five shares, of which the legitimate sons would take four, and so on in the same proportion, whatever number of legitimate sons may be born subsequently.*

A boy adopted by a widow with the permission of her late husband, has all the right of a posthumous son, so that a sale made by her to his prejudice of her late husband's property, even before the adoption, will not be valid, unless made under circumstances of inevitable necessity:† and in the case of a Hindu of Bengal, dying in his father's lifetime without issue, but leaving a widow authorized to adopt a son, if such adoption be made by the widow, with the knowledge and consent of her deceased husband's father, at any time before he shall have made any other legal disposition of the property, or a son shall have been born to his daughter in wedlock, no such subsequent disposition or birth shall invalidate the claim of the son so adopted to the inheritance.‡

The above rules relate to a son adopted in the *Dattaka*

* It is laid down in the *Dattakachandrikd*, that in case of *Sudras*, if a legitimate son be subsequently born he is entitled to an equal share only with the adopted son; and this rule prevails accordingly in the southern provinces.

† Case of Rani Kishermani, *v.* Udwant Singh and another, S. D. A. Reports, vol. iii., p. 220.

‡ Case of Ramkisken Sarkheyl, *v.* Srimati Dibia, S. D. A. Reports, vol. iii., p. 367. See also Colebrooke, in Elem. Hin. Law, App., p. 102.

form. But there is a peculiar species of adoption termed *Dwyámusháyana,* where the adopted son still continues a member of his own family, and partakes of the estate both of his natural and adopting father, and so inheriting is liable for the debts of each. To this form of adoption the prohibition as to the gift of an only son does not apply.* It may take place either by special agreement that the boy shall continue son of both fathers, when the son adopted is termed *Nitya Dwyámusháyana;* or otherwise, when the ceremony of tonsure may have been performed in his natural family, when he is designated *Anitya Dwyámusháyana;* and in this latter case, the connexion between the adopting and the adopted parties endures only during the lifetime of the adopted. His children revert to their natural family.† With a legitimate son subsequently born, the *Dwyámusháyana* takes half a share of his adopting father's property.‡

The question as to the proper age for adoption has been much discussed; and the most correct opinion seems to be, that there is no defined and universally applicable rule as to the age beyond which adoption cannot take place, so long as the initiatory ceremony of tonsure, according to one opinion, and of investiture, according to another, has not been performed in the family of the natural father.

* See the case of Raja Shamshér Mall, *v.* Rani Dilraj Kunwar, S. D. A. Reports, vol. ii., p. 169.

† *Datt. Mim.* Sec. 6, §§ 41 and 42.

‡ *Datt. Chand.* Sec. 5, § 33.

According to the *Dattakamimánsá*, the period fixed beyond which adoption cannot take place is the age of five years; and if the ceremony of tonsure have been performed within that period in the family of the natural father, the son adopted cannot become a *Dattaka* in the ordinary form, but must be considered an *Anitya Dwyámusháyana*, or son of two fathers. This can only be effected by the performance of the sacrifice termed *Putreshti*, by which the son is affiliated in both families.

In the *Dattakachandriká** the period fixed for adoption is extended, with respect to the three superior tribes, to their investiture with the characteristic cords, which ceremony is termed *Upanayana*, and is subsequent to that of tonsure or *Chúrákarana*; and with respect to *Sudras*, to their contracting marriage. But investiture in the one case, and marriage in the other, must be performed in the family of the adopting father. The periods fixed, however, for the investiture of the three superior tribes are different. That of a *Brahmin* should take place when he is eight years of age, which may be construed optionally, as signifying eight years from the date of conception, or from the date of birth. That of a *Khsetriya* at eleven years of age, and that of a *Vaisya* at

* The difference of opinion with respect to this point arises from a difference of grammatical construction. The term in the original is *Chúdádya* (signifying tonsure and the rest), which is a compound epithet termed *Buhobrihi*, which again is divided into two kinds called *tadguna* and *atadguna*, inclusive and exclusive. According to those who adopt the former construction, adoption is lawful even after tonsure; but not so according to those who adopt the latter. The former construction is adopted by *Devándabhatta;* the latter by *Nandapandita.*

twelve. But there are secondary periods allowed: for instance, the investiture of a *Brahmin* may be postponed until sixteen years after the date of conception; and that of a *Kshetriya* until twenty-two years after the same date; and that of a *Vaisya* until twenty-four years. It should be observed, however, that where the ceremony of *Upanayana* has once been performed, an insurmountable bar to adoption is thereby immediately created. Its effect cannot, as in the case of tonsure before the age of five years, according to the authority of the *Dattakamimánsá*, be so far neutralized as to admit of its being re-performed after the ceremony of *Putreshti.**

The authorities being entitled to equal weight in different parts of the country, the only ground of preference must be sought for in the different customs prevailing in different places. In the province of Bengal, and in the southern provinces, the more extended period should be assumed as the limit;† that being apparently consonant to the received practice; while in Benares, the *Dattakamimánsá*, which limits the period of adoption, should for

* This has been doubted by the translator of the *Dattakachandriká* and *Dattakamimánsá*, in his Synopsis at the conclusion of that work, p. 225; and he diffidently expresses his inability to settle the question, though he inclines to the negative: but independently of there being no authority in support of the affirmative of the question, the fact that investiture constitutes a second birth is conclusive against it. Adoption is permitted on the principle that the adopted son is born again in the family of his adopting father; but this cannot be where the investiture, which causes the second birth, has already been performed in the family of the natural father.

† For the doctrine as to the age of adoption according to the southern authorities, see Elements of Hindu Law, p. 75 *et seq.*, and Summary ditto, p. 50.

the same reason be followed. In laying this down as a rule, it may be objected, that there do not exist sufficient grounds for the establishment of its accuracy. It is proper, therefore, that the grounds of the rule should be stated. In the precedents which I have collected, there is no case bearing directly on the point. Case 2. (which is a Bengal case) does not expressly prohibit adoption after the age of five years. And in the case of Keratnarain, *versus* Musst. Bhobinerrí (the only adjudicated one for Bengal that I can find bearing on the question),* the principle of the extended limit was fully discussed and admitted. The limitation to the age of five years is founded on a passage in the *Kalikapuráná*,† and the authenticity of that passage is doubtful. The *Dattakachandriká* makes no mention of it, though the *Dattakamimánsá* does. The latter being a Benares authority, it may be proper to apply the limiting principle to that province, but not to Bengal or the Dekhan, where that principle is not only not recognised, but where it is denied, and adoptions continually take place at an age far exceeding five years. There is no standard work on the subject of adoption expressly for the Bengal school; but whenever there is any difference of opinion between the *Dattakamimánsá* and the *Dattakachandriká*, the doctrine of the latter conforms to that of Bengal; for instance, as to the share to be taken by an adopted with a legitimate son.‡ Other instances might be cited. If it should be considered that the reasons here given are insufficient

* Sadr Diwání Adálat Reports, vol. i., p. 161.

† Digest., vol. iii., p. 228.

‡ *Dáyabhága*, 155.

to warrant the conclusion arrived at, it may at least be contended, that it is open to a Bengal *pandit* to adopt either authority, and that the adoption of that which admits the more extended limit, as being the more liberal construction, could not be objected to. The author of the Considerations on Hindu Law as current in Bengal,* seems averse to the extension of the limit. He maintains, that in the case of Gopímohan Deb, it was the opinion of all the *pandits* who were consulted on his behalf, that proof of his being under the age of five years was indispensable. He also alludes to a remark appended to the case of Keratnarain, *v.* Musst. Bhobinerrí, decided in the S. D. A.; but, with respect to the first, it may be observed, that there does not appear to have been any formal opinion actually taken; and, with respect to the second, it is not apparent from what authority the remark proceeded. The author of the Considerations lays it down as a second rule, that adoption cannot take place in any of the classes after the ceremony of tonsure shall have been performed. From what has preceded, it will appear, however, that "investiture" should have been substituted for the word "tonsure;" and that the doctrine should have been qualified by the provision, that if tonsure had been performed previously to the fifth year, it might be repeated in the family of the adopting father, the adopted son thereby becoming an *Anitya Dwyámushdáyana.* According to the *Mayúk'ha,* an authority of the greatest eminence among the Mahrattas, the restriction as to age relates

* Page 144.

only to the cases where no relationship subsists; but when a relation, or *Sagotra*, is to be adopted, no obstacle exists on account of his being of mature age, married, and having a family.* In Mithilá, where the *Kritrima*† form of adoption prevails, there is no sort of restriction, except as to tribe, it being requisite that the tribe of the adopting father and the adopted son be the same. There is no limit as to age and no condition as to the performance of ceremonies;‡ so much so, that *Keshaba Misra*, in the *Dwaita Parisishta*, treating of this description of adoption, has declared that a man may adopt his own brother,§ or even his own father. But he, as well as his issue, continues after the adoption to be considered a member of his natural family,‖ and he takes the inheritance both of his own family and that of his adopting father.¶ Another peculiarity of this species of adoption is, that a person adopted in this form by the widow does not thereby become the adopted son of the husband, even though the adoption should have been permitted by the husband;** and the express consent of the person nomi-

* Bombay Reports, vol. i., p. 195.

† This form of adoption is wholly unknown in Bengal: but see note, Sutherland's Synop., p. 221, and case of Uman Datt, *v.* Kanhai Singh, Sadr Diwáni Adálat Reports, vol. iii., p. 144.

‡ See the case of Kalian Singh, *v.* Kirpa and another, Sadr Diwáni Reports, vol. i., p. 9.

§ The reverse of this opinion was maintained in the case of Ranjit Singh, *v.* Abhay Narain Singh, S. D. A. Reports, vol. ii., p. 245; but the authorities cited by the law officers in support of the doctrine laid down by them on that occasion had relation to the *Dattaka* form of adoption.

‖ Dig., vol. iii., p. 276.

¶ Sadr Diwáni Adálat Reports, vol. iii., p. 307.

** Ibid., vol. ii., p. 27.

nated for the adoption must be obtained during the lifetime of the adopting party.* This relation of *Kritrima* son extends, as has already been observed, to the contracting parties only; and the son so adopted, will not be considered the grandson of the adopting father's father, nor will the son of the adopted be considered the grandson of his adopting father. He does not inherit collaterally, being ninth in the enumeration, according to *Yájnyawalkya.*†

It has already been observed, that a man who has a son, son's son, or son's grandson, is not competent to adopt a son; and it would seem to follow by analogy, that if a man has a son, and the son of an elder son deceased, he may give the former away in adoption,‡ because he cannot be considered as the father of one son only; the latter also bearing towards him the relation of a son to all intents and purposes, and supplying the place of the elder one. In the *Dattakamimánsá* there is a prohibition against the gift of a son, where there are only two; but the precept is merely dissuasive, and not peremptory.

Two persons cannot join in the adoption of one son. A notion seems to have prevailed, that two brothers might adopt the same individual; but this is entirely erroneous.§ The supposition seems to have proceeded

* Sadr Diwání Adálat Reports, vol. iii., p. 173.

† Dig., vol. iii., p. 276.

‡ In this case the dissuasive precept against giving one of two sons would apply, but the adoption would nevertheless be valid.

§ See Considerations on Hindu Law, p. 473, *et seq.*

on a misconstruction of the following text of *Manu*:— "If among several brothers of the whole blood, one have a son born, *Manu* pronounces them all fathers of a male child by means of that son."* But that text is not meant to authorize the adoption of a nephew even, by two or more brothers. The adopted son of one brother would of course offer up oblations to the ancestors of all, and so far would perform the office of a son to them also; but he would not take the estate of his adopting father's brothers, in the event of their having any nearer heir.

Another point which has been the subject of much discussion is, as to whether an adopted son by the *Dattaka* form succeeds collaterally, as well as lineally; but this may now be said to be set at rest, and decided in the affirmative. It is true that *Jimútaváhana*, in the *Dayabhága*, has contended that the son adopted in the *Dattaka* form cannot succeed to the property of his adopting father's relations; but the doctrine being in opposition to the text of *Manu*, cannot be held entitled to any weight.† It should be observed, however, that a son so adopted has no legal claim to the property of a *Bandhu* or cognate relation; for instance, if a woman on whom her father's estate had devolved, adopt a son with the permission of her husband, the son so adopted will not be entitled to such estate, on his adopting mother's death. It will go to her father's

* Cited in Dig., vol. iii., p. 266.

† This question has been amply discussed in the Considerations on Hindu Law, p. 128 *et seq.* See also case of Shamchandra and Rúderchandra *v.* Narayaní Dibia and Ramkisheu Rai, S.D.A. Reports, vol. iii., p. 128.

brother's son, in default of nearer heirs. This point was determined in a case recently decided by the court of Sadr Diwání Adálat.* It is not quite evident why a daughter's adopted son should be excluded from inheriting the estate of his adopting mother's father, while a son's adopted son's right of succeeding collaterally has been acknowledged, inasmuch as the maternal grandfather is enumerated among the kindred by all the Hindu legislators; but the reason is, that the party adopted in the latter case becomes the son of a person whose lineage is distinct from that of the maternal grandfather.

The difference of opinion existing as to whether a *Dattaka* should be considered as heir of the adopter's kinsmen or not, arises from a difference in the order of enumeration in the twelve descriptions of sons; some legislators maintaining, that *Manu* included the *Dattaka* among the first six, who are entitled to inherit collaterally, while others maintain that the same lawgiver ranked him among the last six, who can only inherit lineally. In the *Dwaita Nirnaya* the several opinions have been noticed, and the author of that work gives his own in favour of the *Dattaka*. In Sir William Jones's translation of the Institutes of *Manu*, the *Dattaka* is ranked among the first six; and a great majority of the *pandits* throughout the country who were consulted on the subject when it was agitated in the Supreme Court, expressed their opinion, that the *Dattaka* is entitled to inherit

* See the case of Ganga Maya, *v.* Kishen Kishore and others, S.D.A. Reports, vol. iii., p. 128.

collaterally.* The author of the *Dattakachandriká*, according to his usual expedient of reconciling conflicting doctrines, puts the decision of the question on the character of the claimant—a criterion, it must be confessed, not very precise.†

It is clear, that a man having adopted a boy, and that boy being alive, he cannot adopt another. It is written in the *Dattakamimánsá*: "A man destitute of a son (*aputra*) is one to whom no son has been born, or whose son has died; for a *text of Saunaka* expresses, 'one to whom no son has been born, or whose son has died, having fasted for a son, etc.:'‡ but it seems to be admitted, that a man having a legitimate son may not only authorise his wife to adopt a son after his death, failing such legitimate son, but also, failing the son so adopted, to adopt another in his stead;§ and

* This question was circulated by the court of Sadr Diwání Adálat to all the courts under its jurisdiction, to ascertain the law on the point from their Hindu law officers. See p. 161, Considerations on Hindu Law.

† The author has here inserted an important report on a complicated case of adoption which will be found at the end of the chapter.—W.

‡ Page 2.—There is a *vyavasthá* maintaining the opposite doctrine, the authority cited for which is a verse ascribed to *Manu*, though not to be found in the Institutes: "Many sons are to be desired, that some one of them may travel to Gaya." But this text obviously relates to legitimate sons. See the case of Gaurípershad Rai, *v.* Jymala, p. 136, vol. i., S. D. A. Reports. And Mr. Colebrooke observes, in a note to p. 42, ibid., that the validity of a second adoption, while another son, whether by birth or adoption, is living, is a question on which writers of eminence have disagreed; that *Jagannáthá* in his Digest, inclines to hold it valid; but that the author of the *Dattakamimánsá*, a work of great authority, maintains the contrary opinion.

§ Case of Shamchandra and Rúderchandra, p. 209, vol. i., S. D. A. Reports, where it was established, that there may be two successive adoptions by the widows of the same man; and the case of Musst. Súlakhna, *v.* Ramdulal Pande and others, p. 324, vol. i.

it has also been ruled, that authority to a wife to adopt, in the event of a disagreement between her and a son of the husband, then living, will not avail; though authority to adopt, in the event of that son's death, would be valid.* It is a disputed point, whether a widow having, with the sanction of her husband, adopted one son, and such son dying, she is at liberty to adopt another without having received conditional permission to that effect from her husband. According to the doctrine of the *Dattakamimánsá*, the act would clearly be illegal; but *Jagannáthá* holds that the second adoption in such case would be valid, the object of the first having been defeated. According to the authorities in Bengal and Benares, a woman is competent, after the death of her husband, to adopt a son, provided he gave her permission to do so during his lifetime, and according to the law of the western provinces, with the sanction of the husband's kindred, after his death; these authorities contending, that although a woman cannot of herself perform the ceremonies requisite to adoption, yet that there is no objection to her calling in the assistance of learned Brahmins, as is practised by *Sudras* on similar occasions. But according to the doctrine of *Vachaspati*, whose authority is recognized in Mithilá, a woman cannot, even with the previously obtained sanction of her husband, adopt a son after his death, in the *Dattaka* form; and to this prohibitory rule may be traced the origin of the practice of adopting

* Case of Musst. Súlakhna, *v.* Ramdulal Pande and others, vol. i., p. 325.

in the *Kritrima* form, which is there prevalent. This form requires no ceremony to complete it, and is instantaneously perfected by the offer of the adopting, and the consent of the adopted party. It is natural for every man to expect an heir, so long as he has life and health; and hence it is usual for persons, when attacked by illness, and not before, to give authority to their wives to adopt. But in Mithilá, where this authority would be unavailable, the adoption is performed by the husband himself; and recourse is naturally had to that form of adoption which is most easy of performance, and therefore less likely to be frustrated by the impending dissolution of the party desirous of adopting.

It is an universal rule in Bengal and Benares, that a woman can neither adopt a son, nor give away her son in adopting, without the sanction of her husband previously obtained; but it does not appear that the prohibition in Mithilá, which prevails against her receiving a son in adoption according to the *Dattaka* form, even with the previous sanction of her husband, he being dead, extends to her receiving a boy in adoption according to the *Kritrima* form: and the son so adopted will perform her obsequies, and succeed to her peculiar property, though not to that of her deceased husband.* It is not uncommon in the province of Mithilá for the husband to adopt one *Kritrima* son, and the wife another.

* Suth. Synopsis, note 5, p. 222.

I have laid it down as a rule, that in the present age, adoption is allowable only in the *Dattaka*, *Dwyámusháyana*, and *Kritrima* forms: but I find, on reference to the Elements of Hindu Law, that a question was agitated as to the admissibility of the *Kritra*, or son bought. The point was much canvassed, and gave rise to a protracted controversy between two of the most eminent scholars of the day;* and there is a case in the Sadr Diwání Adálat Reports,† in which the claimant was alleged to be of the *Paunarbhava* class:‡ and in which in all probability the claim would have been adjudged, had it been proved to be customary for sons of that description to succeed. Although, therefore, it may be asserted, that generally speaking, there are only three species of adoption allowable in the present age, yet the rule should be qualified, by admitting an exception in favour of any particular usage which may be proved to have had immemorial existence. Thus it appears that the *Goswámis*, and other devotees who lead a life of celibacy, buy children to adopt them in the form termed *Krita*, or son bought; and that the practice of appointing brothers to raise up male issue to deceased, impotent, or even absent husbands still prevails in Orissa.§ The son so produced is termed *Kshetraja*, or son of the wife; and doubtless these several sorts of subsidiary sons should be held entitled to the patrimony of their adopting fathers, in places where the

* See Elem. Hin. Law, App., p. 107 *et seq.*

† Vol. i., p. 28.

‡ See *Mitak.*, chap. i., sect. 2, § 8.

§ Note to Dig., vol. iii., p. 276.

lex loci would justify the affiliation.* In former times, it was the practice to affiliate daughters, in default of male issue; but the practice is now forbidden.† The other forms of adoption enumerated by *Manu*‡ appear to be wholly obsolete in the present age. Any discussion, therefore, of their relative merits would be foreign to the purpose of this publication.

APPENDIX.§

I may here be permitted to introduce the following report of a case decided on the 30th April, 1821, tending to establish the point of collateral succession and as generally connected with the law of adoption. The report was not given with other decisions of the S. D. A. of the same year; and from the importance of the case, it may be concluded that the omission was attributable to oversight.

The appellant in this case was Gaurharí Kabiraj, guardian of Sheopershad Chowdharí, a minor, against Musst. Ratneswarí Dibia, mother of Karuna Kant Rai, also a minor.

The suit was originally instituted by the appellant against Kasí Kant Rai, in the Moorshedabad provincial court, on the 14th of March, 1814, to recover possession of a three-anna share of the *zemindarí*, Pargana Tahirpúr,

* See note S. D. A. Reports, vol. ii., p. 175.

† *Jimútaváhana*, cited in Digest, vol. iii., p. 493.

‡ Institutes, chap. iv., §§ 159 and 160.

§ The case here transferred from the text p. 83, will afford a good specimen of the Reports of the Sadr Diwání Adálat, so often referred to.—W.

and the independent Kismats Talgachí, Jagannathpúr, etc., etc.,, in *zila* Rajshahi. The action was laid at Rs. 7051, the estimated annual produce.

The plaint set forth, that Raja Mahendranarayan had five sons, viz., Ramendranarayan, Rabíndranarayan, Jádabendranarayan, Maníndranarayan, Upendranarayan, of whom Jádabendranarayan and the two others last mentioned, died without children. On the death of Mahendranarayan, one moiety of the six-anna share in Pargana Tahirpúr, which constituted his *zemindari*, descended to Anandendranarayan, the adopted son of Ramendranarayan and father of Sheopershad, a minor, and the other half to Bhairabendranarayan, as heir to his adopting father Raghúindranarayan, son of Rabíndranarayan. Amendendranarayan Chowdharí sold a five-pie share of his three-anna portion, and retained possession of the remaining portion. Bhairabendranarayan died in 1204 B.S., leaving Jagadíswarí his wife, and Banmálí Dibia his daughter. Jagadíswarí obtained possession, and was registered as proprietor of her husband's share: and in the year 1212 B.S., gave Banmálí, when she was nine years old, in marriage to the defendant. Banmálí died on the 27th of Phalgun, 1213 B.S., before she arrived at years of maturity; and Jagadíswarí likewise died on the 17th of Chait, in the same year. As Sheopershad was entitled to perform the *sráddha* and to succeed to the property left by Jagadíswarí, he presented a petition to the collector to be registered as proprietor of the deceased's estate, which was opposed by the defendant on the plea that Jagadíswarí had made a gift in 1207 B.S., of the *zemindari* and her other property to him and to his wife Banmálí, to which he was therefore entitled: his claim was also opposed by Iswarchand, a person who represented himself to be the adopted son of the deceased, and who likewise applied for the entry of his own name. The collector rejected Sheopershad's application, and ordered the defendant's name to be entered for Jagadíswarí's *zemindari*, according to the conditional deed of gift produced by him, though contrary to the *shastras*, and referred Sheopershad and Iswarchand to a civil suit. Iswarchand brought an action in the *zila* court, through his guardian Gangaram Bhadarí, and obtained a decree, which was reversed on appeal by the provincial court, and his claim as adopted son rejected. This decision was subsequently affirmed by the Sadr Diwání Adálat, which court passed an order, on the 4th of February, 1813, directing Sheopershad to prefer his claim, as heir, either in the *zila* or provincial court, to the estate left by Jagadíswarí, when it would be decided whether the deed of gift produced by Kasí Kant Rai was valid or not, according to the *shastras*. Banmálí Dibia was married to Kasí Kant in the year 1212 B.S., and the deed of gift produced by the defendant as having been executed by Jagadíswarí in favour of himself (Kasí Kant) and his wife Banmálí is dated the 3rd of Asharh, 1207 B.S. Jagadíswarí was in possession of the estate during her lifetime, namely, till Chait, 1213 B.S., during which time Kasí Kant Rai (who was not competent to perform the exequial rites) had nothing to do with it, and no mention was made of the deed of gift. From the condition specified in the said deed, it appeared that the gift was made to

Kasí Kant and Banmálí Dibia, in the event of the latter becoming pregnant. It was very suspicious, and altogether unlikely that the idea of Banmálí's pregnancy should have been entertained five years previous to her marriage, and inserted in the deed of gift. The instrument by which Jagadíswarí bequeathed her property on her death to the defendant and Musst. Banmálí is invalid, inasmuch as she is not empowered by the *shastras* to alienate it by sale or gift, and as, moreover, Banmálí died during the lifetime of Jagadíswarí, her succession was thereby defeated. Besides, by a compromise entered into formerly between Anandendranarayan, the father of Sheopershad, and Bhairabendranarayan, the husband of Jagadíswarí, it was provided that the estate and property of either of them who should die without children should go to the survivor and his heirs; so that in every point of view, Sheopershad was entitled to Jagadíswarí's property.

The defendant, in answer, stated that after three of the five sons of Raja Mahendranarayan had died without children, Rabíndranarayan, grandfather of Bhairabendranarayan, the husband of Rani Jagadíswarí, and Ramendranarayan, grandfather (as alleged by the plaintiff) of Sheopershad, became possessed of the six-anna share of Pargana Tahirpúr. A moiety, or three-anna share devolved at the death of Rabíndranarayan on Raghúindranarayan by the law of inheritance, and on his death it went to Bhairabendranarayan, and on his dying without sons to his widow Musst. Jagadíswarí. The remaining three-anna share descended to Anandendranarayan, by a gift from Rani Súkhí, widow of Ramendranarayan, and a deed of compromise alleged to have been executed by Bhairabendranarayan. The property did not go to Anandendranarayan by right of adoption; for Raní Súkhí, after her husband's death, had in conformity to his permission, adopted in the first instance a person named Rúdranarayan, and on his death, Anandendranarayan, without the permission of her husband, and in opposition to the *shastras*, on which account she had made a gift to him of her estate. An adoption of this nature has never been recognized by the *shastras*, by the usages of the Brahmins and other Hindu tribes. A suit was in consequence instituted in the *zila* court between Bhairabendranarayan and Anandendranarayan, and regularly carried in appeal before the Sadr Diwání Adálat. The *vyavasthá* submitted by the Pandit of the *zila* court, which likewise coincided with five legal opinions filed by Bhairabendranarayan, invalidated the adoption. The *zila* judge, however, acted on the opinion expressed by other Pandits, which were submitted by Anandendranarayan, and passed a decree in his favour, declaring in that decree, which was dated June the 30th, 1795, that the object of Raní Súkhí in executing a deed of gift of that nature, was to secure to Anandendranarayan in some way, either by adoption or by gift, the succession to her property, and that in event of any dispute arising after her death on the subject of the second adoption, there might be no doubt of her property descending to Anandendranarayan under the deed of gift. By the decision of the superior court the adoption of Anandendranarayan was declared illegal, and he was allowed to succeed to the property solely on the ground of the deed of gift and the compromise, the authenticity of which was not ascertained. Besides, even supposing the adoption to have been valid, the person adopted is only entitled to the property of his adopting father, and has no claim to the property of his adopting father's family or collateral relations. Sheopershad, therefore, could have no title whatever to the three-anna share of the estate in dispute. The following, he affirmed, was the true state of the case. It is the usage among Brahmins for a *Kúlín*, when he marries into an inferior family, to receive a large valuable consideration. Accordingly, in 1207 B.S., Raní Jagadíswarí, wife of Bhairabendranarayan, who was of an inferior family, having agreed to give her daughter Banmálí Dibia in marriage to him (defendant), who was of the *Kúlín* caste, made a gift of her zemindarí and other property to his wife Banmálí Dibia and himself, with the knowledge and consent of all her family, as well as of Anandendranarayan. But in consideration of their youth, she executed an *ikrárnama* in the form of a will, in favour of his (the defendant's) father, Kalí Kant Rai, empowering him to superintend and take care of the estate during the period of their minority, and died in the year 1213 B.S. Anandendranarayan also lived to 1212 B.S., subsequent to the execution and registry of the deed of gift, and had he considered himself the heir of Raní Jagadíswarí, he would undoubtedly have opposed the proceeding, either at the time or at some subsequent period of his life. He, however, had never done so. On the death of Raní Jagadíswarí, Gangaram Bhadarí, the plaintiff's uncle, having persuaded Benúd Ram Rai, proprietor of a ten-anna share in the above *Pargana*, to collude with them, forged an *ijazatnama*, or deed of permission to adopt, and a *hibbanama* and other documents, and sued him (the defendant), first stating that Iswarchandra was the adopted son of the Raní: but their claim was rejected, and, therefore, the present suit (fraudulently preferred on the ground that Sheopershad was the heir, and entitled to the property alienated by the gift of the Raní) was altogether inadmissible; inasmuch as the illegality of Anandendranarayan's adoption invalidated the claim of Sheopershad to the property of Raní Jagadíswarí; and the Raní having before the birth of Sheopershad, made a gift of her property to him (the defendant) and to his wife, it could not be considered as her estate on her death. Besides, he had himself, with his own money, paid off a mortgage contracted on the estate since the time of Bhairabendranarayan when it would otherwise have been sold. The forgery of the deed of compromise produced by the plaintiff was evident, from the circumstance of its being dated on the 11th of Bhadún, 1212 B.S. The suit about the adoption of Anandendranarayan, pending between him and Bhairabendranarayan, his (the defendant's) father-in law, was decided in the Rajshahí *zila* court on the 13th of Asharh in the above year, afterwards in the provincial court, and lastly in the Sadr Diwání Adálat on the 4th of Aswin 1208 B.S. Had the deed of compromise been genuine and in the possession of Anandendranarayan, he would undoubtedly have brought it forward in some court of justice. And as the cause between Anandendranarayan and Bhairabendranarayan was pending till 1208 B.S., it was extremely improbable that a compromise should have been entered into in 1202 B.S.

Anandendranarayan also was a minor at that time, and many suits had been preferred in the civil and criminal court and in the collector's office relative to the estate between 1202 and 1213 B.S., a period of twelve years, during which Rani Jagadíswarí was alive; but no mention had ever been made of the compromise, nor had it ever been registered, or before produced.

On the death of the defendant, his wife Musst. Ratneswarí Dibia, mother of Karuna Kant Rai, his minor son, became his representative in the suit.

The plaintiff, in replication, maintained that Ramendranarayan, grandfather of the minor Sheopershad, and his brother Rabíndranarayan lived together as members of an undivided family. Rabíndranarayan died leaving a son, Raghúindranarayan, his heir; and Ramendranarayan died leaving his widow, Musst. Lakshmíswarí, to whom he granted permission to adopt a son. In Kartik 1170 B.S.: Raghúindranarayan died leaving a widow, Musst. Saraswatí, who with Lakshmíswarí, the grandmother of the minor Sheopershad, enjoyed joint possession of the estate. Musst. Saraswatí adopted Bhairabendranarayan, entered his name jointly with that of Lakshmíswarí, in the collector's office, and died in 1162 B.S.: and the grandmother of Sheopershad died after having adopted Anandendranarayan according to her husband's permission, put him in possession of the estate during her own lifetime, and by means of an application effected the registry of his name instead of her own. Bhairabendranarayan afterwards instituted an action on the ground that the adoption of Anandendranarayan was illegal. By the decisions, however, of the *zila* and provincial courts and of the Sadr Diwání Adálat, the adoption of Anandendranarayan was held to be valid, and a decree passed in his favour. There could, therefore, be no doubt of Sheopershad's title, and of his being *Pindádhikár*, or person entitled to perform the exequial rites of Jagadíswarí and Bhairabendranarayan. As Kalí Kant Rai, father of Kasí Kant, the defendant, was adopted by Kishen Kant Rai, and according to the *shastras* the distinction of the Kúlín caste is lost on the adoption, and as the dignity of the ancestors of Mahendranarayan (who were Rajas) was superior, the allegations of the defendant relative to Jagadíswarí having given her property to him on his marriage with her daughter, in consideration of his rank, were evidently false, inasmuch as from the time of the ancestors of Mahendranarayan, Ramendranarayan, and Anandendranarayan, connexions had existed between them and the Kúlín Brahmins. No one ever gave his whole estate to his daughter and son-in-law, but it is both the law and usage, that if a person dies without male issue, his estate will not devolve to his daughters or daughter's sons, but only to the descendants from the same grandfather. In accordance with this custom, on the death of Indranarayan Rai without male issue, his estate did not go to Ramsingh, his daughter's son, who was alive, but to the persons descended from the same grandfather as himself. The truth of all these representations will be established on inquiry. If the father of Sheopershad had been aware of the gift alleged by the defendant, he would certainly have opposed it. It is singular that the deed of gift declares, that the gift is made for the performance of exequial ceremonies, and stipulates that Rani Jagadíswarí, shall, during her lifetime, retain possession of the above estate, and have the power of alienation by sale or gift. As, therefore, the Rani enjoyed possession of the estate, and retained the power of disposing of it by gift or sale; and did, subsequently to the execution of the deed of gift, give, in the exercise of her proprietary right, *devottar* and *brahmottar* lands to many persons, and the donee did not obtain possession of the lands given to him, it did not clearly appear with what view the will in favour of the defendant's father was executed, or what law legalized a conditional gift of the above nature, or how, Banmálí Dibia having died childless in the lifetime of her mother, the condition relative to the performance of exequial ceremonies could hold good.

The rejoinder of Ratneswarí Dibia set forth, that as both the donor and the donee were dead, and the property given had descended as an hereditary estate, the claim of any person thereto was inadmissible according to the *shastras*; and that her son as the *Pindádhikár* of Banmálí Dibia, was undoubtedly entitled to her property. On the 13th of June, 1817, the second judge of the provincial court dismissed the claim with costs, on the ground of the *vyavasthá* submitted by the *pandit* of the court which declared that an adopted son was entitled to the property of his adopting father, not to that of his adopting father's collateral relations; that a woman had not the power to adopt a second person on the death of an individual whom she had previously adopted, with her husband's permission; and that, therefore, Anandendranarayan and consequently Sheopershad, were not entitled to the property in dispute; and that the deed of gift executed by Jagadíswarí in favour of Banmálí Dibia and Kasí Kant, her daughter and son-in-law, was valid.

The appellant being dissatisfied with this decision, appealed to the court of Sadr Diwání Adálat, laying his claim at Rs. 15,151, three times the *sudder jama* of the lands in dispute.

Iswarachandra Rai, the person claiming to have been adopted by Rani Jagadíswarí, presented a petition to the following effect.

"The suit instituted by Gangaram Bhadarí, your petitioner's guardian, against Kasí Kant, to effect the reversal of the acting collector's order for the registry of Kasí Kant's name as proprietor of a three-anna share in the *zemindari* Pargana Tahirpúr, was decreed by the judge of *zila* Rajshahí. This decision was, however, reversed in the provincial court, and the order of the provincial court was affirmed on the 4th of February, 1813, by W. E. Rees, Esq., formerly acting judge of the Sadr Diwání Adálat. On your petitioner making frequent applications for redress to the former judges of this Court, he was informed by Mr. Harrington, that when the cause of Sheopershad Chowdharí came before the court, they would take into consideration your petitioner's case and decide upon it. As your petitioner's adoption is established by the papers in the case of Sheopershad, *v.* Kasí Kant (No. 1779), your petitioner hopes, that when the above cause comes before you, you will take into consideration the present petition, and the papers filed on the former trial, as well as the petitions for a review, and the *vyavasthás* of the *pandits* of this court filed in the cause of Raní Siromaní and others, and afford him redress."

The case having been brought to a hearing before the second judge (C. Smith), all the pleadings and exhibits of the parties were perused, as well as two petitions presented by Iswarachandra Sarma, two *vyavasthás* of the *pandits* of this court, one in the case of Bijia Bibia, appellant, *v.* Annapúrna Dibia, respondent, the other in the case of Shamchandra Chowdharí, and Rúdra Chandra Chowdharí, appellants, *v.* Narayaní Dibia Chowdharain and Ramkishore Rai, respondents, and the interrogatories of this court to the *pandits* aforesaid; the papers of the Rajshahi *zila* court, the provincial court, and the Sadr Diwání Adálat in cause (No. 846), of Gangaram Bhadarí, guardian of Iswarachandra Sarma, appellant, *v.* Kasí Kant Rai, respondent, and the decrees passed by all those three courts therein. Copies of two *vyavasthás* of the *pandits* of this court filed by the appellant's *vakil,* and the proceedings in three different suits, viz., Bijia Dibia, appellant, *v.* Annapúrna Dibia, respondent; Sehan Lal Khan, appellant, *v.* Raní Siromaní, respondent; and Iswarachandra Pal and others, appellants, *v.* Krishen Govind Sein, respondent.

The *vyavasthá* of the *pandits* in the case of Shamchandra and Rúdrachandra, delivered on the 21st of August, 1807, was to the following effect.

Q. Subsequently to the death of Krishenkishore, his senior widow had adopted Nandkishore as a son, and on the death of the son so adopted, the second widow of the said Krishenkishore adopted an individual called Ramkishore, who is still living: under these circumstances, Júgalkishore, a person adopted by Krishengopal, the uterine brother of Krishenkishore, and his half brother Lakshminarayan's two sons, Shamchandra and Rúdrachandra, claim the property left by Nandkishore and Krishenkishore: Now supposing the adoption of both the sons to have been proved, in this case, which of the claimants is or are entitled to inherit the property of Kishenkishore and Nandkishore? and does an adopted son succeed collaterally as well as lineally?

R. The property whether consisting of moveables or immoveables, belonging to Krishenkishore deceased, who left no issue of the body, will devolve on the son whom his younger widow had adopted according to the mode prescribed by law. The uterine son adopted by Krishenkishore's brother and his half brother's sons have no right of succession. The property of the deceased Nandkishore, in default of issue of his adopting mother, will devolve on the adopted son of his step-mother whom she adopted with her husband's sanction, provided he be endued with the requisite qualities, and able to benefit his parents by performing the (*Nitya*) indispensable and fixed observances, (*Naimittika*) casual rites (*Kamya*) supererogatory works (which are performed at pleasure, or through the desire of some advantage), (*Ishta*) essential ceremonies, as ablution, investiture, etc., (*Púrtta*) acts of pious liberality, as digging a well, planting a grove, building a temple, etc., and so forth, prescribed to his own tribe. In this case, the surviving adopted son (of the second widow) being a nearer *Sapinda* to the deceased son adopted (by the eldest widow) than the other relations who claim, he will succeed exclusively to the property, and the kinsmen will have no claim. This opinion is consonant to the doctrine of *Manu*, *Gautama*, and *Bodháyana*, the first of whom holds the first rank among legislators; and the doctrine is also consonant to the *Manwartha Múktavali*, *Dattakamimánsá*, *Vivadabhangárnava*, *Ratnákara*, and other authorities.

Authorities.—The text of *Devala* cited in the *Dáyatatwa* and other tracts: "All these sons are pronounced heirs of a man who has no legitimate issue by himself begotten." The passage of *Yajnyawalkya* cited in the *Dáyatatwa* and other law books: "The wife and the daughters, also both parents, brothers likewise."

"Of him who leaves no son, the father shall take the inheritance, or the brothers." *Manu*. The Text of *Vrihaspati* cited by *Raghunandana* and others:—"*Manu* holds the first rank among legislators, because he has expressed in his code the whole sense of the *Vedas*, and no code is approved which contradicts the sense of any law promulgated by *Manu*." The texts of *Manu* laid down in the Ratnákara and other tracts:—"Of the twelve sons of men, whom *Manu*, sprung from the self-existent, has named, six are kinsmen and heirs; six not heirs, except to their own father, but kinsmen. The son begotten by a man himself in lawful wedlock, the son of his wife begotten in the manner before mentioned, a son given to him, a son made or adopted, a son of concealed birth, or whose real father cannot be known, and a son rejected by his natural parents, are the six kinsmen and heirs." "*Manu*, sprung from the self-existent *Brahma*, and first of the fourteen *Manus*; among these twelve sons of men whom he has named, the first six are pronounced kinsmen and heirs to collaterals; the result is, that, as kinsmen, they offer the funeral cake and water to *Sapindas* and *Samánodakas,* and, as heirs, they succeed to the heritage of their collateral relations, on failure of male issue, as well as to the estate of their father." This is the explanation of *Kullúkabhatta.* The following texts are laid down in the *Ratnákara* and other tracts. *Gautama* :—"The son begotten by a man himself in *lawful wedlock,* the son of a wife *begotten by an appointed kinsman,* a son given, a son made by adoption, a son of concealed birth, and one rejected by his natural parents, are sons who inherit property. The son of an unmarried girl, the son of a pregnant bride, a son by a twice-married woman, the son of an appointed daughter, a son self given, and a son bought, claim the family of their adopting fathers."

Bodháyana :—"Participation of wealth belongs to the son begotten by man himself *in lawful wedlock,* the son of his appointed daughter, the son begotten on his wife *by a* kinsman *legally appointed,* a son given, a son made *by adoption,* a son of concealed birth, and a son rejected *by his natural parents.* Consanguinity *denoted by a common family appellation,* belongs to the son of an unmarried girl, the son of a pregnant bride, a son bought, a son by a twice married woman, a son self given, and a son of a priest by a *Sudra.*" Although *Jimútaváhana, Raghunandana,* and others, explaining the text of Devala cited in the Dáyabhága, have not reconciled the dispute in regard to the given son and the rest being heirs to collaterals or otherwise, yet it should not therefore be supposed that the given son has no right of collateral succession. The difference of opinion may be reconciled by referring to the distinction of the adopted son being (*Saguna*) endued with good qualities, or (*Nirguna*) not so endued. This is the doctrine contained in the *Ratnákara* and other authorities; and it must be admitted that the given son and the rest who are endued with good qualities, are entitled to succeed both to the adopting father and his kinsmen. It is also proper to affirm, as intended by that expression, that sons given and others, being virtuous, are entitled to the inheritance and so forth, in preference to a son by a twice married woman or the like, if he be destitute of good qualities; but if all be destitute of good qualities, he who is superior as nearest allied by birth, shall take a full share of the paternal estate, and the rest shall have the portions allotted to them in the *Brahmapurana* and other works.

The maintenance directed must consist in the receipt of such a share; else the *seeeming* contradiction in the texts of *Manu* and others, and of *Yajnyawalkya* and the rest, could not be well reconciled. But some argue, from the concurrent import of the text of *Devala*, that the text of the *Brahmapurana* also relates to sons given and the rest, who are inferior in class to their adoptive fathers.—*Vivádabhangárnava.*

The vyavasthá in the case of Bijia Dibia against Annapúrna Dibia, was to the following effect.

Q. Taraní Chowdharain having, at her husband's death, taken possession of his entire property, real and personal, selected for adoption a boy named Kalikant, with her late husband's sanction. It appears from the deposition of a witness Bhavanisankar, adduced by Kalibhairab and the said Taraní (who were defendants in this cause) that Kalikant died previously to the celebration of the ceremonies prescribed for adoption; but it appears from the statement of the plaintiff Bijia Dibia, that the boy died subsequently to his adoption. A few years after his death, the said Taraní assigned over all the property which she held in her possession to her junior daughter's son (Kalibhairab), while her senior daughter was living and had a daughter. Subsequently the senior daughter was delivered of a son, who laid claim to a moiety of the property disposed of as above stated. Under these circumstances, was the said Taraní, according to the law of Bengal, competent to give away all her husband's property to her daughter's son, while she had another daughter living, and is the deed of gift in such case valid and binding? Supposing the adoption of Kalikant to have been actually made in this case, was she (the said Taraní) competent, after the death of such adopted son, to dispose of her adopted son's property by deed of gift in favour of her daughter's son?

R. A widow, without sanction of her husband's representatives, is incompetent to make a gift of his property, which had devolved on her by right of inheritance, and the deed of gift which she made cannot be considered as valid or binding. No adopting woman is allowed to dispose of her adopted son's property which had devolved on her at his death, by a deed of gift in favour of one heir, while there is a possibility of the birth of another. This opinion is conformable to the *Dáyabhága*, *Dáyanirnaya*, *Dáyarahasya*, *Vyavasthárnava*, *Dáyatatwa*, and other authorities current in Bengal.

Authorities.—"But the wife must only enjoy her

husband's estate after his demise. She is not entitled to make a gift, mortgage, or sale of it." Thus Katyáyana says: "Let the childless widow, preserving unsullied the bed of her lord, and abiding with her venerable protector, enjoy with moderation the property until her death. After her, let the heirs take it." "Abiding with her venerable protector:" that is, with her father-in-law, or others of her husband's family, let her enjoy her husband's estate during her life; and not as with her separate property, make a gift, mortgage, or sale of it at her pleasure. The *Dáyabhága.* It is laid down in the *Dáyanirnaya,* that "no widow is competent to make a gift, or mortgage, or sale of her husband's property, except for the sake of performing his exequial rites, or other necessary purpose; and she residing with her husband's family is entitled to consume only such portion of his estate as may suffice for her subsistence."

For women, the heritage of their husbands is pronounced applicable to use. Let not women on any account make waste of their husband's wealth. The *Bharata.* By the word "waste" it is meant, that a woman cannot make a gift, sale or other alienation of her husband's property at her pleasure. The *Dáyarahasya.*

"The property of a person dying, leaving neither son, son's son, nor son's grandson, goes to his virtuous widow; but she cannot make any alienation, as sale or the like, of such property, excepting for the purpose of promoting her husband's spiritual benefit by giving a part of it, or for the purpose of saving her own life." The *Vyavasthárnava.*

The text of *Náreda* laid down in the *Dáyarahasya:*—"Every sort of contract made by a woman, not in a time of distress, is null and void, particularly the gift, mortgage, and sale of the house and field."

The word "wife" is employed as a term of general import: and implies that the rule must be understood as applicable generally to the case of a woman's succession by inheritance. The *Dáyabhága.*

The following passage is cited in the *Dáyabhága* and *Dáyarahasya*:—"They who are born, and they who are yet unbegotten, and they who are actually in the womb, all require the means of support; and the dissipation of their hereditary maintenance is censured."

The second judge recorded his opinion on the 2nd of January, 1821, in these terms:—

"I am of opinion that neither of the parties in the present case is entitled to the property left by Rání Jagadíswarí, inasmuch as it has been established that Iswarachandra Chowdharí, the appellant in the cause (No. 846), is the rightful heir. The proofs in favour of such a conclusion are fully detailed in my proceeding of this date. If, in concurrence with me, the Court, after admitting a review of judgment in case No. 846, reverse the decisions of this Court, and of the provincial court, and affirm the decree of the Rajshahí *zila* court, it will be necessary to affirm the decree passed by the Múrshedabad provincial court in this case. If, however, on the contrary, they uphold the decree passed by this Court on the 4th of February, 1813, I consider the title of Sheopershad Chowdharí (appellant) to be, according to the *Shastras*, undoubtedly superior to that of Kasíkant Rai, the respondent's father. For Kasíkant Rai only stood in the relation of a son-in-law which ceased on his wife's dying without children during her mother's lifetime, and his claim under the conditional deed of gift is altogether inadmissible according to the law of inheritance; inasmuch as the condition was cancelled by the death of the person on whom the fulfilment was enjoined, and on failure of Raní Jagadíswarí's own and adopted children Sheopershad Chowdharí, the appellant, appears the only person who has any title to succeed as heir." Under these circumstances, the second judge recorded his opinion, that the Court should either admit a review of judgment in Iswarachandra Chowdharí's case, reversing the decrees of this, and of the provincial court, and affirming the decree of the Rajshahí *zila* court, dated July the 12th, 1808, and uphold the decision of the first judge of the Múrshedabad provincial court, dated June 13th, 1817, dismissing Sheopershad's claim, and making the costs of all courts payable by the parties respectively; or that they should reject the application for a review in case No. 846, and, affirming this Court's decree dated on the 4th of February, 1813, should reverse the decision of the first judge of the Múrshedabad provincial court, and award to Sheopershad Chowdharí, a three-anna share of *zemindarí* of Pargana Tahirpúr, with mesne profits for the period during which it had been in the possession of Kasíkant Rai, charging the costs of both courts to the respondent.

The case was next brought before the third and officiating judges (S. T. Goad and W. Dorin). Their proceeding of the 8th of February was to the following effect.

"It appears that the appellant lays claim to a three-anna share in the *zemindari* of Pargana Tahirpúr, which was in the possession of Rani Jagadíswarí, who died in 1213 B.S. The Raní was seized of the three-anna share in dispute on the death of her husband Bhairabendranarayan in the year 1204, who left no male issue and only one daughter. The daughter also died at the age of nine or ten years, after her marriage with the late Kasíkant Rai, the respondent's husband. The appellant maintains that the share in dispute being the estate left by Bhairabendranarayan, the husband of Jagadíswarí, descends to his heir, and as he is the son of Anandendranarayan, Bhairabendranarayan's uncle who was adopted by Raní Saraswati and was likewise the second adopted son of Raní Lakshmí, he is entitled to it according to the law of inheritance. The respondent contends, that Raní Jagadíswarí transferred the above estate to her daughter and the husband of that daughter by a deed of gift executed on the 23rd of Asharh, 1207 B.S., under the expectation that her daughter would bear a son, stipulating that she (the donor) should remain in possession of the lands during her lifetime, as she accordingly did for six or seven years, and she opposes the claim preferred on the grounds of hereditary right by the appellant,

1st. Because the adoption of Anandendranarayan by Raní Lakshmí the wife Ramendranarayan had not taken place according to the *Shastras*.

2nd. Because, even if the adoption of Anandendranarayan had been legal, the appellant's claim to succeed as heir to the estate of Bhairabendranarayan and Raní Jagadíswarí was inadmissible according to the *Shastras*, inasmuch as he could not claim relationship with the husband of Raní Jagadíswarí through the adoption of his father.

But with respect to the objections urged by the respondent to the legality of Anandendranarayan's adoption by Raní Lakshmí, in conformity to the permission of her husband, it is only necessary to state that Anandendranarayan died in 1212 B.S., till which time he was in possession of his adopting father's estate, and that it appears from a decree passed by this Court on the 28th September, 1801, in the case of Raní Jagadíswarí, appellant, *v.* Anandendranarayan, a minor, respondent, that several objections raised to the adoption of Anandendranarayan were overruled at the time by this Court, and the adoption declared to be valid. Bhairabendranarayan, moreover, the husband of the appellant upon that occasion, admitted the legality of the adoption. Adverting to the foregoing circumstances, the Court do not consider that the respondent is authorized, after so great lapse of time, now to call in question the legality of Anandendranarayan's adoption. And as it is evident, from several *vyavasthás*, that the deed of gift executed by Raní Jagadíswarí for her husband's estate, to the possession of which she had succeeded on his dying without male issue, is perfectly invalid, it only remains to ascertain whether now the appellant is, according to the Hindu law, entitled to the estate in dispute as heir."

A copy of this proceeding was accordingly ordered to be laid before the *pandits* of the Court, together with the genealogical table furnished by the appellant, to enable them, after a due consideration of their contents, to submit within a fortnight a *vyavasthá* consonant to the Hindu law as current in Bengal, in reply to the following question.

Q. If the deed of gift produced by the respondent be illegal, and at the death of Jagadíswarí her husband's heirs had the right of succeeding her, in this case is the appellant, according to the law of Bengal, entitled to the property in question by right of representation or otherwise?

R. Although Bhairabendranarayan should have died leaving no issue but a daughter, and his property should have been enjoyed by his widow Jagadíswarí during her life, and the deed of gift (produced by the respondent) of all her property in favour of her daughter and her husband be illegal, yet on her demise her property, even though it be subject to the succession of her husband's heirs, will not devolve on the appellant; for he cannot claim it by right of representation, as he being the son of Anandendranarayan, the second adopted son of Lakshmí Dibia, does not hold the rank of a *Sapinda.* A person according to law may desire his wife to adopt his son, but neither by law nor custom can he direct her to adopt one, and after his death another. The second adoption by the widow must be considered as illegal, and the adopted son cannot thereby rank in the relation of *Sapinda;* and it follows *à fortiori* that the appellant has no tie of relationship with the deceased, when his father is debarred from that right. It appears in the question, that Bhairabendranarayan acknowledged the adoption of Anandendranarayan; and the Court, having rejected the objections expressed on the subject, admitted the adoption to be good and legal. The ruling authority is independent, and may act according to its pleasure; but according to law, the second adopted son can be entitled to inherit the property of the individual only by whom he is adopted, and cannot inherit the property of his adopting parent's *Sapindas*. This opinion is consonant to the *Dattakamimánsá*, *Dattakachandriká*, *Vyavaháramátriká*, and other authorities as current in Bengal.

Authorities:—The texts laid down in the above authorities: "By a man destitute of a son only, must a substitute for the same always be adopted: with some one recourse (*Yasmáttasmát* prayatnatas) for the sake of the funeral cake, water, and solemn rites. 'The funeral cake:' 'the *Sráddha*, or funeral repast." 'Water:' that is, the presenting water in the two united palms, and so forth. 'Solemn rites:' meaning rites in honour of the deceased, cremation and the like. These are the cause (*hetu*). The reason, occasioning the adoption, is the cause. This, from being used in the singular number, shews that these ceremonies collectively are the cause, and not individually; and consequently, the meaning is, that there is not a distinct affiliation, severally for each; but one adoption only, on account of the whole: for on default of a son, the failure of the oblation of food and other rites is the consequence." The *Dattakamimánsá*.

As, in their proceedings of the 8th of February, 1821, the Court did not require the *pandits* to give an opinion as to the legality or illegality of the adoption of Anandendranarayan, they were directed to refrain from all consideration of the merits of that question; and taking for granted that it was legal, and that Anandendranarayan was the adopted son of Rani Lakshmí, wife of Ramendranarayan, to submit, within three days a specific answer to the question proposed in the proceeding of the above date. It was added, that the Court would again take into consideration what was stated in their former *vyavasthá* relative to the adoption of Anandendranarayan after their delivery of the second *vyavasthá.* On the 21st of March, 1821, the required reply was submitted, and was to the following effect.

"Suppose the Court to determine that the adoption of Anandendranarayan by Raní Lakshmí, the widow of Ramendranarayan, was valid, yet, as it was a second adoption, he (Anandendranarayan) could not be considered a *Sapinda* of Bhairabendranarayan, nor *à fortiori* could his son Sheopershad be considered a *Sapinda* of the said Bhairabendranarayan. Therefore, if after the death of Raní Jagadíswarí, the widow of Bhairabendranarayan, the property which had devolved on her at his death is to descend to her husband's heirs, Sheosherpad cannot have any right of succession."

As it appeared that the *pandits* had still not given an explicit reply to the question propounded by the Court in their proceeding of the 8th of February, they were directed to give their opinion *de novo,* taking for granted that the adoption of Anandendranarayan was valid and unobjectionable in every respect, and as if Anandendranarayan were the sole adopted son of his adopting father; and the following was the purport of the third *vyavasthá,* submitted on the 3rd of April, 1821: That if Anandendranarayan was the sole adopted son of his adopting father, and there was otherwise no question as to the legality of his adoption, in such case he must be considered as a member of the *Gotra* of his adopting father, and legally entitled to the property of his adopting father's *Sapindas*; and in the event of there being no nearer *Sapinda* to Bhairabendranarayan, than the appellant Sheopershad, in such case the said appellant must be considered entitled to the estate. The *pandits'* opinion proceeded in the following manner:—This opinion is conformable to *Manu*, although the Court directed that our *vyavasthá* be according to the law of Bengal; and of all the authorities, the Dáyabhága is there the most prevalent: and, although it is the opinion of *Jimûtaváhana*, quoting the text of *Devala*, and adopting his order of enumeration, that the son affiliated in the *Dattaka* form is not an heir of collateral relations (Sapindas, etc.), nevertheless, as many *vyavasthás* have been delivered in the Court establishing the adopted son's collateral succession according to the law promulgated by *Manu*, this opinion is delivered according to the same law. Authorities:—*Manu*: "Of the twelve sons of men, whom *Manu*, sprung from the self-existent, has named, six are kinsmen and heirs; six not heirs, *except to their* own father, but kinsmen. The son begotten by a man himself in *lawful wedlock*, the son of his wife begotten *in the manner before mentioned*, a son given to him, a son made or *adopted*, a son of concealed birth, *or whose real father cannot be known*, and a son rejected *by his natural parents*, are the six kinsmen and heirs." Commentary on the text of *Manu* by *Bálambhatta*: "*Manu*, sprung from the self-existent *Brahma*, and first of the fourteen *Manus*; among those twelve sons of men whom he has named, the first six are pronounced kinsmen and heirs to collaterals: the result is, as kinsmen, they offer the funeral cake and water to *Sapindas* and *Samánodakas;* and as heirs, they succeed to the heritage of their collateral relations, on failure of male issue." The text of *Manu*, laid down in the *Dáyabhága*, *Dáyatawa*, *Dáyakramasangraha*, and other authorities: "To the nearest kinsman (*Sapinda*) the inheritance next belongs."

On the receipt of the above *vyavasthá*, the Court observed, that from this *vyavasthá* it appeared, that in consequence of the death of Rání Jagadíswarí, widow of Bhairabendranarayan, without male issue in 1213 B.S., her husband's estate, which had been enjoyed by her during her lifetime, would descend to her husband's nearest heir; and supposing Anandendranarayan to have been the adopted son of Ramendranarayan and Rání Lakshmí and a member of the family, that Sheopershad, the original plaintiff in the present cause, would succeed hereditarily as a *Sapinda*. In concurrence, therefore, with the opinion expressed by the second judge, they passed a decree in favour of the appellant's claim, reversing the judgment of the Múrshedabad provincial Court, and making the costs of both Courts payable by the respondent. By the decree possession of the three-anna share in dispute, was awarded to the appellant, with the mesne profits from the date on which the suit was instituted till put in possession. The following observations were introduced into the final decree.

It must be remembered that the proceeding of this Court under date the 8th of February last, declared the respondent disqualified to call in question on the present occasion the legality of the adoption of Anandendranarayan, the appellant's father, inasmuch as the legality of that transaction had been admitted, and recognized by a decree passed by the Sadr Diwání Adálat on the 28th of September, 1801, (which corresponds with 1208 B.S.) in the case of Raní Jagadíswarí, appellant, *v.* Anandendranarayan, respondent. It appears, moreover, that Anandendranarayan was adopted in 1200 B.S., by Raní Lakshmí and enjoyed possession of his adoptive father's estate till his own death in 1212 B.S., when he was succeeded by his son, who, as heir, continued in possession until the institution of the present suit in 1220 B.S. The same objection now urged to the adoption was preferred on the former trial, viz. that the adoption, by the wife of any *zemindar*, of a second son, after the death of a previously adopted individual, was invalid. Two of the soundest and most learned *pandits* of the day, however, viz. those of the Tirhút and Nadia *zila* Courts, who were called on to submit their opinions on the subject, pronounced, in concurrence with the *pandit* of the Rajshahi *zila* Court, the adoption to have been a legal transaction; and as the former judges of this Court in 1801, by their decree admitted and decided on the legality of Anandendranarayan's adoption in face of the alleged objection, the Court was of opinion that the above-mentioned decree, and the long lapse of time, does not leave the question of law open to their investigation. From the former decree of this Court, the grounds on which the judgment pronounced on that occasion was formed cannot be ascertained. But it is doubtful whether the former Court considered the adoption of Anandendranarayan as a second adoption effected by Raní Lakshmí without permission from her husband, and legalized it, proceeding on the *Ijazatnama* obtained by her from her husband, although it specified no permission for adopting a second person, or construing the tenor of the *Ijazatnama* to imply a tacit consent to the adoption of a second, on the death of the first son, which frustrated and nullified the object of the adoption, or whether they considered that the ceremonies of adoption had not been completely fulfilled in the case of the first son; for he died a few months afterwards, and according to the testimony of several witnesses, before he had gone through the ceremonies of investiture. Yet although these circumstances have not been detailed, it is evident that by that decree the adoption of Anandendra-narayan, which it must be observed is nowhere described therein as a second *adoption*, was declared legal after a due consideration of all the objections urged, and he was pronounced a member of the family. The question of law, therefore, is quite irrelevant to the present case. The *Shastras* were merely consulted to ascertain whether the appellant Sheopershad, being descended from the same paternal grandfather, was entitled by the law of inheritance, to the estate in dispute; and the Court, in deciding that he is so entitled, have been guided by the above legal opinions and the *vyavasthá* submitted by the *pandits* in the case of Shamchandra and others, appellants, *v.* Narayaní Dibia, respondent. There are certain other points which the Court consider it advisable to notice here.

1st. The authorities cited in the first *vyavasthá* submitted in this cause do not affect the adoption of two sons by one wife of a deceased husband, or even a second adoption generally; nor is such an allegation supported by the tenor of former *vyavasthás*, furnished by the *pandits* in the cases of Shamchandra and other appellants *v.* Narayaní Dibia, respondent; and Gauríprasád Chowdharí, appellant, *v.* Mussammat Jymála, respondent.

2nd. The respondent's *vakíl*, after the *vyavasthá* was submitted, and while the cause was still pending, only contended that the adoption was illegal, inasmuch as it had taken place without the consent of the husband.

3rd. In the proceedings of this Court, and in the question propounded to the *pandits*, only the word "adoption" was at first mentioned: the word "second" was subsequently added at the request of the respondent's *vakíl*, as it was thought that it would not materially affect the decision. It was, however, mentioned, that according to the evidence, it was doubtful whether the ceremonies of adoption in the first case were regularly fulfilled.

CHAPTER VII.

OF MINORITY.

AGREEABLY to the Hindu law, as current in the Benares and Mithilá schools, minority is held to last until after the expiration of sixteen years of age;* and according to the doctrine of Bengal, the end of fifteen years is the limit of minority.†

A father is recognized as the legal guardian of his children, where he exists; and where the father is dead, the mother may assume the guardianship:‡ but where the duties of manager and guardian are united, she is, in the exercise of the former capacity, necessarily subject to the control of her husband's relations: and with respect to the minor's person likewise, there are some acts to which she is incompetent, such as the performance of the several initiatory rites, the manage-

* "Until the minors arrive at years of discretion:" in the sense of restriction, before they attain their seventeenth year. The Ratnákara. See Dig., vol. iv., p. 243. According to Colebrooke, sixteen years must be completed.—Elem. Hin. Law, App., p. 208.

† See Annotations on the *Dáyabhága*, p. 58, and Dig., vol. i., p. 300.

‡ And this has been held to include the step-mother, whose right of guardianship was declared to be superior to that of the minor's paternal uncle.—Bombay Reports, vol. ii., p. 144.

ment of which rests with the paternal kindred. In default of her, an elder brother of a minor is competent to assume the guardianship of him. In default of such brother, the paternal relations generally are entitled to hold the office of guardian, and failing such relatives, the office devolves on the maternal kinsmen, according to their degree of proximity, but the appointment of guardians universally rests with the ruling power.*

The guardianship of a female (whether she be a minor or an adult) until she be disposed of in marriage, rests with her father: if he be dead, with her nearest paternal relations.† After her marriage, a woman is subjected to the control of her husband's family. In the first instance, her husband is her guardian: in default of him, her sons, grandsons and great grandsons are competent to assume the guardianship; and in default of them, her husband's heirs generally, or those who are entitled to inherit his estate after her death, are competent to exercise the duties of guardian over herself and her property. On failure of her husband's heirs, her paternal relations are her guardians; and failing them her maternal kindred. In point of fact, females are kept in a continual state of pupilage.

The ruling power is in every instance, whether the natural and legal guardians be living or dead, recognized to be the legitimate and supreme guardian of the property

* Dig., vol. iii., p. 544, Elem. Hin. Law, App., 202.

† See App. Elem. Hin. Law, p. 22 and 204.

of all minors, whether male or female:* and it may here be mentioned, that agreeably to the regulations of government, the state of minority is held to extend to the end of the eighteenth year.†

As to the power of guardians over the property of their wards, I apprehend that much misapprehension exists. As I understand the provisions on the subject, "Minors are under the protection of the law; favoured in all things which are for their benefit; and not prejudiced by any thing to their disadvantage."‡ It has been laid down by Sir William Jones, that "assets may be followed in the hands of any representative."§ This is doubtless true, but a latitude has been given to the rule which the terms of it do not warrant. It has been held, I believe, that for this purpose, a guardian may be considered as the representative of the deceased: whereas it is obvious, that *quoad hoc*, he is only the representative of his successor. I understand the expression to mean, that whoever takes the assets, whether near or remote in the order of inheritance, is liable for the debts of the deceased, so far as those assets go,

* Thus the property of a woman, and the goods of a minor, falling into the king's power, should not be taken by him as owner: this has been already noticed. But it may be here remarked, that the property of a minor should be entrusted to heirs, and the rest *appointed* with his concurrence; or if the infant be absolutely incapable of discretion, with the consent of a near and unimpeachable friend, such as his mother and the rest. See Dig., vol. iv., p. 243.

† Sect. 2, Regulation XXVI. 1793.

‡ Colebrooke on Obligations and Contracts, chapter x., § 585.

§ See note to Colebrooke's Translation of Jagannátha's Digest, vol. i., p. 266.

provided such heir have attained the age of majority; and that, where the heir is a minor, the creditor must wait until the minority expires before he can come upon the assets for the liquidation of his debts. Subject to this condition, the son must pay his father's debts, as well as all necessary debts contracted on his account during his minority. And according to the Benares school, the debts of the father are binding on the son,* whether the former left property or not, as well as those of the grandfather; but he need not pay interest on the latter. The following case arose but very lately in the court of Sadr Diwání Adálat. A, a Hindu *zemindar* of Bengal, executed a deed of sale for a portion of his estate to B; B executing a separate engagement that the sale should be redeemable by repayment of the money with interest within the term of a year. Before the term expired, the *zemindar* A died, leaving a widow and an adopted minor son, or rather a son adopted by authority, after his death, by the widow. Within a few days of the completion of the term when the sale would have become absolute and irrevocable, the widow, as guardian of the minor, borrowed money elsewhere of C, with which she paid the debt of B and freed the land, executing to the

* But the obligation is considered only as a moral and not a legal one, provided there are no assets. See Colebrooke, cited in App. Elem. Hin. Law, p. 347; but the same high authority has laid it down as a principle, in his treatise on obligations and contracts (chap. ii., § 51), that heirs succeed to the obligations of ancestors without any reference to the adequacy of the property, and the rights of inheritance must be relinquished, when its obligations are repudiated. And see Elem. Hin. Law, App., p. 464 and 465.

lender a similar second sale of the same land, redeemable within a given term; which term, however, expired without repayment on her part. The question then here was, first, Could any rule of Hindu Law prevent the land becoming the property of B, on the term of the first sale expiring without repayment? Secondly, If there be no such rule, and the widow saved the land for a time by the second conditional sale, was it not a case of necessity, such as to justify her act in behalf of her ward as clearly beneficial to him? Thirdly, If a father sell a portion of his land, with a condition for redemption, and his heir (a minor), or his guardian on his part, do not redeem, is not such land gone irrevocably? And fourthly, Do the debts of a father become payable out of his assets, even in the hands of his heir (who is a minor), on demand from the guardian? The substance of the reply of the Hindu law officers consulted on this occasion was, that no necessity for the sale had been made out, inasmuch as the estate of the deceased could not have been legally alienable for his ancestor's debts until after the minor had attained majority. Judgment was, however, given for the purchaser, and the following arguments were used on the occasion: That supposing the ancestor's conditional sale to have remained unredeemed after the expiration of the period stipulated, and the usual term of notice, the land would, of necessity, have fallen to the former creditor: That it was mere folly to urge, that the act of the mother in saving it for a time, and obtaining a further period, was not to be held good as an act evidently for the benefit of the minor, inasmuch as, but for her renewal by a fresh loan in her capacity of guardian, the conditional sale must undoubtedly have become absolute to the creditor: That according to the invariable practice of the courts, no plea of minority could be listened to, or any other doctrine recognized than that the estate of a Hindu of Bengal becomes liable at his death for his just debts, especially where he has pledged his land as security for those debts, and that his power of selling outright or conditionally, any part of or all his landed property, could not be questioned: That any other doctrine would involve in confusion the acts of the Court for many years past, as there was scarcely a contract of conditional sale in the provinces where that form of contract prevails, in which some one of the numerous co-sharers were not minors when the sale became absolute; and that if their minority, in such cases, must be considered a bar to foreclosure, and cause the transaction to run on fifteen years longer, there would probably be an end to such transactions altogether, and it would not be possible to raise money at all, or at least not except on harder terms than the present: That the doctrine maintained by the Court appeared to be supported by the opinion of the commentator *Jagannátha*,* and that, though there should prove to be conflicting opinions as to the law, the established usage and practice ought to prevail. And, in short, that whatever might be

* See Digest, vol. i., chap. 5, on payment of debts, and particularly text 172, as translated by Mr. Colebrooke.

the real doctrine of the Hindu law on the subject, the Court was bound to follow that law in matters of inheritance, marriage, caste and religious usages only, and not in matters of contract, of which nature the case in question appeared to be.

In answer to the above arguments, it may be observed, that supposing the minor's estate not to be liable, there did not exist any necessity for the widow's making a conditional sale. It may be assumed too, that according to our own regulations, a mortgage would not be foreclosed against a minor, and that he would be allowed his equity of redemption on coming of age. It did not, therefore, signify whether the term of the mortgage was near expiring or not. It was at the lender's own risk to take a mortgage, in which the borrower's interest might expire before the expiration of the term.

I shall not, however, enter into any question as to the expediency or otherwise of the doctrine established in this instance, but content myself with a brief inquiry as to the law of the case, which appears quite clear, when disencumbered of the commentary of *Jagannátha*, whose authority cannot be held to be oracular or incontrovertible in any instance, especially where it is opposed by texts of unquestioned weight and indubitable import. The first text at all to the point is that of *Yajnyawalkya* (191). It has thus been translated by Mr. Colebrooke, with a view to adapt it to the subsequent commentary of *Jagannátha*. "He who has received the estate of a proprietor, leaving no son *capable of business*, must pay the debts *of the estate*, or on failure of him, the person who takes the wife of the deceased; but not the son whose father's assets are held by another." Now here it must be observed, that the words in *Italics* are not in the original, and that the expression "capable of business" is clearly an interpolation of the commentator. The original is *rikthagrahi*, or taker of the property. In the concluding part of the text it is distinctly stated, that the son whose father's assets are held by another must not pay the debts. The next text is that of Náreda (172), which agreeably to Jagannátha's comment, has been thus translated by Mr. Colebrooke: "If the successor to the estate, the guardian of the widow and the son not *competent to the management of affairs*, he who takes the assets becomes liable for the debts; the son, *though incompetent*, must pay the *debt* if there be no guardian of the widow, nor a successor of the estate; and the person who took the widow, if there be no successor of the estate, nor competent son."

Here the original does not mean a son incompetent from minority to manage his affairs, but a son incompetent to inherit by reason of some natural disqualification, such as blindness, disease or the like. A son, even though incompetent to inherit, in the same manner as a son who does not inherit assets, is morally bound to pay his father's debts; and the object of the above text is to show the obligation under which he lies, if there be no successor to the estate, nor guardian of the widow. There is nothing whatever, in any text that I have been able to discover, relative to the payment of debts by a guardian. Lastly come the two texts of *Katyáyana* and Náreda (187 and 188). "On the death of a father, *his debt* shall in no case be paid by his sons, incapable from nonage of conducting their own affairs; but at their full age of *fifteen years*, they shall pay it in proportion to their shares, otherwise they shall dwell hereafter in a region of horror." "Even though he be independent, a son incapable from nonage of conducting his affairs is not *immediately* liable for debts." It will be observed that *Jagannátha*, in commenting on these passages, attempts to make a distinction between minority and infancy, and infers that it is only during the latter state that a son is exempted from liability for his father's debts; but the text in the original is *apráptavyaváhara*, which clearly means one who has not attained the age prescribed for the management of affairs. It follows, that where, owing to a son's minority, the father's assets are taken in charge by another person, such person cannot legally apply any portion of the assets to the payment of the father's debts; and that it is only where a person succeeds to property in his own right, that he is at liberty to pay the debts of the ancestor by means of such property. A guardian may, indeed, dispose of a portion to meet a necessity arising for the minor's subsistence; but no necessity can by possibility arise for disposing of any portion to pay the minor's father's debts, for he must cease to be a minor before he can be liable. Nor does there appear to be much of hardship in this rule. The provisions of the English law savour of much more hardship; for, according to it, real estates are not subject at all to the payment of debts by simple contract, unless made so by will. All immoveable property, in the Hindu law, is subject to a kind of entail; so much so, that the right of the son is equal to that of the father, supposing the property to be ancestral: and it would be hard enough, under such circumstances, that the imprudence of the father should ruin the son; for, as it is, he is bound, both legally and morally, to pay the debts: and it may be, perhaps, but just, that the period for exacting payment should be postponed until he comes to years of discretion sufficient to enable him to realize the means of satisfying the creditors with the least detriment to himself. The assets cannot in the mean time be alienated by the minor, and the creditor is ultimately sure, where assets exist, of receiving the amount of his demand with interest. Especially in a case of mortgage, where the produce of the property on usufruct might be awarded to the creditor in lieu of interest, which arrangement could not operate prejudicially to either party, or involve any breach of the Hindu law, for the usufruct of property is one species of legal interest which is called *bhogalábha*, or interest by enjoyment. The *pandits* being called upon to expound the law in a case involving a similar question* which was recently decided at Bombay, they declared that a woman who had succeeded as heir at law, to property left by her own father, cannot dispose of that property in liquidation of the debts of her husband, unless her son, having already attained the age of sixteen years,

* Bombay Reports, vol. i. p. 176.

or age of discretion, shall consent to the act. This it will be observed, is a stronger case than the one above alluded to, because a son is bound to pay the debts of his father, whether he inherit assets, or not; and by this decision it was determined, that property to which he had a claim in expectancy only, could not be alienated for that purpose, until he attained the age of majority; and it has been ruled also, in a case decided under the Madras presidency, that the father being dead, his son is not liable for his debts until after he has attained the age of seventeen.*

* Elem. Hin. Law, App. p. 206.

CHAPTER VIII.

OF SLAVERY.

SLAVERY, among the Hindus, cannot properly be enumerated among their religious institutions. In the year 1798, the Court of Sadr Diwání Adálat, with reference to the long established and sanctioned usage of slavery in these provinces, stated their opinion, "that the spirit of the rule for observing the Mohammadan and Hindu law, was applicable to cases of slavery, though not included in the letter of it." And this construction was confirmed by the Governor-General in Council, on the 12th of April, 1798; but it was at the same time admitted, that the rule in question is not directly and strictly applicable to questions of personal freedom and bondage.* It will suffice, therefore, in this place, to give a general outline of the subject, which cannot be done in more comprehensive language than has been already employed by Mr. H. T. Colebrooke.† He observes, "the Hindu law fully recognizes slavery. It specifies in much detail the various modes by which a

* Harington's Analysis, note 3, p. 70, vol. i.
† Cited in Ibid. vol. iii. p. 743.

person becomes the slave of another, and which are reducible to the following heads, viz. capture in war, voluntary submission to slavery for diverse causes (as a pecuniary consideration, maintenance during a famine, etc.); involuntary for the discharge of debt, or by way of punishment for specific offences; birth, as offspring of a female slave; gift, sale, or other transfer by a former owner; and sale or gift of offspring by their parents. It treats the slave as the absolute property of his master, familiarly speaking of this species of property in association with cattle under the contemptuous designation of 'bipeds and quadrupeds.' It makes no provision for the protection of the slave from the cruelty and ill-treatment of an unfeeling master; nor defines the master's power over the person of his slave;* neither prescribing distinct limits to that power, nor declaring it to extend to life or limb. It allows to the slave no right of property, even in his own acquisitions, unless by the indulgence of his master. It affords no opening to his redemption and emancipation (especially if he be a slave by birth or purchase), unless by the voluntary manumission of him by his master, or in the special case of his saving his master's life, when he may demand his freedom,†

* It will be seen, from the case of slavery (Precedents, No. 9), that the *pandits* of the Sadr Diwání Adálat when consulted on the subject, did not hesitate to assign limits to the master's power over the person of his slave; but in the delivery of their opinion they were probably guided by reason, rather than by express law, or perhaps from the analogy of the rule with respect to servants, *Manu*, Dig., vol. ii., p. 209.

† But in this instance *Jagannátha* makes a distinction. In vol. ii., p. 242, he gives the following illustration: "where a slave, neglecting his own safety, and highly valuing his master's life, rescues him from the encounter

and the portion of a son; or in that of a female slave bearing issue to her master, when both she and her offspring are entitled to freedom, if he have not legitimate issue; or in the particular instances of persons enslaved for temporary causes (as debt, amercement, cohabitation with a slave, and maintenance in consideration of servitude), on the cessation of the grounds of slavery, by the discharge of the debt or mulct, discontinuance of the cohabitation or relinquishment of the maintenance." Those slaves who correspond to the designation of *adscripti glebae*, or hereditary serfs, and who, according to the same eminent authority,* are common in the upper provinces, are subject to the laws of ancestral real property, and cannot be transferred except under similar restrictions. Over land acquired by the grandfather, over a corrody and other slaves employed in the husbandry, says *Yájnyawalkya*, the father and the son have equal dominion.† All other descriptions of slaves would appear to class with personal property. The question of ameliorating the condition of slaves in India has not escaped the consideration of Government; but the difficulty of legislating on so delicate a subject must be obvious. Every one who has had the good fortune to be born in a state of freedom must be sensible of its invaluable blessings, and

of a tiger or the like, and is himself preserved by the act of God; in that case he is released from slavery. But if some person attempt to destroy a man by poison, and the slave of that man discovering it, prevent him from eating the poisoned food; or if a master intended to go out of his house, not aware of a tiger standing at the door, but his slave, seeing the tiger, prevent him; in these and similar cases, it may be admitted he is not released from servitude.

* Ibid. 745. † Cited in Dig., vol. ii. p. 159.

numerous arguments will occur to every mind in favour of the abolition of slavery. That the evils of slavery are manifold, is unquestionable. That its total and immediate suppression might be followed by mischievous consequences, can admit but of as little question; while in India it must be confessed, whatever objections may be theoretically advanced to its existence, the condition of the slave himself differs in not much more than in name from that of a hired servant. Speaking of the Mohammadan slavery in another place,* I have observed: "In India (generally speaking) between a slave and a free servant there is no distinction but in the name, and in the superior indulgences enjoyed by the former: he is exempt from the common cares of providing for himself and family: his master has an obvious interest in treating him with lenity; and the easy performance of the ordinary household duties is all that is exacted in return." I have no reason to believe that the system of slavery, as it exists among the Hindus, is productive of much individual misery, however baneful its effects may be to society at large. The courts of justice are accessible to slaves as well as to freemen, and a British magistrate would never permit the plea of proprietary right to be urged in defence of oppression. If, then, but few grievances are complained of, it is fair to infer that few exist.

It was one of the suggestions of the philanthropic individual † who advocated the cause of the abolition of

* Prelim. Rem. Prin. and Prec. Moh. Law.

† Mr. Richardson, formerly judge and magistrate of Bundelkhand, who in the year 1810, submitted the draft of a regulation on the subject.

slavery in India, that, in the event of its being deemed inexpedient to suppress the system altogether, the Mohammadan law, as being more lenient in its provisions, should be universally adopted, to the exclusion of that of the Hindus. But to the latter class, it is evident that the standard of the former would not admit of adaptation; for, according to the Múselman tenets, they only are, legally speaking, slaves, who are captured in an infidel territory in time of war, or who are the descendants of such captives. Capture in war is indeed a cause of slavery according to the Hindu law, as well as according to the Mohammadan; and perhaps among all other nations, the same cause was originally productive of the same effects. The triumph of the strong over the weak destroys the natural equality of the human condition; and to a savage mind, the persons of the conquered obviously suggest themselves as the legitimate reward of victory. To this source in all countries may be traced the privation of freedom. But with the gradual increase of civilisation, when superiority of physical force alone became less respected, other causes operated to the establishment of servitude of a more or less qualified nature; and thus with the Hindus, besides the right accruing from conquest, and transfer implying a previously existing right (which comprehends the *Grihajata*, or one born of a female slave in the house of her master; the *Krita*, or one bought; the *Labdha*, or one received by donation, and the *Kramágata*, or one inherited from ancestors), there is that species of slave termed *Atmavikrita*, or one self-sold, signifying him who for a pecuniary consideration barters his own freedom. All the slaves above enumerated, and their offspring, must be considered to be in a state of permanent and hereditary thraldom.

There exists, besides, the state of bondage in various temporary forms, many of them differing slightly, if at all, from voluntary servitude. One who offers himself willingly as a slave, he who was won in a stake, and even a captive in war, may effect their own emancipation, by offering a proper substitute.* One who enters into a state of slavery for the sake of maintenance, and he who becomes a slave for the sake of his bride, may both be restored to freedom, on relinquishing the object which induced them to part with it.† A pair of oxen is the price of emancipation to one maintained in a famine: while one relieved from a great debt, and he who has been pledged for a certain sum, or hired for a specific period of slavery, are emancipated, the two former on payment of the consideration and the latter on the expiration of the term.‡ An apostate from religious mendicity, is he who forsakes his duty and deviates from the rules of the order which he has imposed on himself, as if he were to take a wife, or otherwise act like a householder, § in which case he should be condemned to a state of slavery; but it is inferrible, that the offence may be expiated by the payment of a fine. ||

From the above it will be perceived, that there are five descriptions of permanent thraldom, from which emancipation can be effected only at the will and pleasure of the master, and that four of those five are consequent on a pre-existent state of slavery. For the rest, on performance

* *Náreda*, cited in Dig., vol. ii., p. 246 † *Náreda*, ibid., p. 247.
‡ *Náreda*, ibid., pp. 243, 247. § Dig., p. 227. || Ibid., p. 229.

of certain conditions peculiar to each, the slave is entitled to freedom.

It must be owned, that the recognition of legal slavery in any form must tend to perpetuate its existence; but at the same time, long-established usages should be respected, especially where society has not attained such a state of civilisation, as to admit of a clear perception of the general benefits intended to result from an invasion of individual rights: and so long as the legislature, in its wisdom, and from a respect for ancient institutions, shall not deem it advisable to interfere with a view to the suppression of the system, it can only be hoped that the gradual diffusion of knowledge, and the consequent spread of enlightened notions, will tend to convince all ranks of the community, that rational liberty is the condition most conducive to the happiness and interests of mankind.*

* There are nine cases illustrative of the doctrine of slavery given in the second volume of the original work. The question appears also to have been a good deal discussed in the courts subordinate to the presidencies of Madras and Bombay. See Elem. Hin. Law, App., p. 230, *et seq.*

After a laborious investigation into the condition of slaves in India, the results of which were printed by order of Parliament, an act was passed by the Government of India, Act V. of 1843, by which cognizance of the condition of a slave in any case was withdrawn from the Company's courts and no such distinction for the future admitted.—W.

CHAPTER IX.

OF CONTRACTS.

THE principles of the Hindu law relative to contracts are founded on the basis of good sense and equity. The same incapacitating circumstances which are the means of avoiding contracts, according to other systems, have been specified by the Hindu jurists. Thus, insanity, minority, coverture, lesion, error, force, fraud, incompetency, incapacity, and revocation,* are each the cause of effecting the dissolution of obligations. To these must be added degradation, entry into a religious order,† and any predicament that operates as a civil death.

The term insanity comprehends not only madmen and idiots, but also all those who labour under any species of fatuity, and who are naturally destitute of power to discriminate what may and may not be done.‡ Minority

* *Vrihaspati*, cited in Dig., vol. ii., p. 328. *Manu*, ibid., vol. i., p. 458.

† *Vasishtha*, ibid., vol. iii., p. 327.

‡ Dig., vol. ii., p. 187. There is a case detailed in the Bombay Reports (vol. ii., p. 114) in which the sale of a house by an aged, infirm, and foolish man was set aside at the suit of his wife, upon a *vyavasthá* of the Hindu law officers, the price paid being proved to be inadequate, though it was not by any means established that the vendor was an idiot.

continues until after a man has entered his sixteenth year, when he becomes acquainted with affairs, or *adult in law*;* but in the Hindu law, minority is used as a term of indefinite import, and comprehends those who are incapacitated from conducting their own affairs by extreme old age, as well as those who are incapable owing to their extreme youth.†

The Hindu law recognizes the absolute dominion of a married woman over her separate and particular property, except land given to her by her husband. He has, nevertheless, power to use and consume it in case of distress; and she is subject to his control, even in regard to her separate property.‡ It is a general rule, that coverture incapacitates a woman from all contracts; but those contracts are valid and binding which are made by wives, the livelihood of whose husbands chiefly depends on their labour; § so also are those made for the support of the family during the absence or disability, mental or corporeal, of the husband. ||

A contract, says *Manu*, "made by a person intoxicated, or insane, or grievously disordered, or wholly dependent, by an infant, or a decrepid old man, or *in the name of another* by a person without authority, is null." In these cases, lesion may be presumed on the ground of incompetency. But among persons who are

* *Smriti*, cited in Dig., vol. ii., p. 115. † Dig., vol. ii., p. 187.
‡ Colebrooke, Obl. and Con. Book iv., 6, § 611.
§ Dig., vol. i., p. 318; and see case 2, Chap. of Debts, vol. ii.
|| Dig., vol. i., p. 296.

competent, the maxim of "*caveat emptor*" applies. Thus, *Náreda* ordains: "A buyer ought at first himself to inspect the commodity, and ascertain what is good and bad in it; and what after such inspection he has agreed to buy, he shall not return to the seller, *unless it had a concealed blemish.*"* There is indeed a provision similar to that which obtains in the Mohammadan law, giving an option of inspection; and with respect to articles not of a perishable nature, the contract may be rescinded within ten days.† For other articles of a perishable nature, there are different periods allowed, subject to the payment of a small fine by the rescinding party.‡

A gift may be revoked, if made under a mistake; and by analogy to this rule, every contract is vitiated by error.§

Any species of duress vitiates a contract. Thus *Jagannátha*, commenting on the text of *Náreda*, to the effect that what a man does while disturbed from his natural state of mind is void, observes: "In cases of fear and compulsion, the man is not guided solely by his own will, but solely by the will of another. If, terrified by another, he give his whole estate to any person for relieving him from apprehension, his mind is not in its natural state; but after recovering tranquillity, if he give anything in the form of a recompense, the donation is valid.‖ This corresponds with

* Cited in Dig., vol. ii., p. 313. † *Manu.* ‡ Dig., vol. ii., p. 321.
§ Colebrooke, Obl. and Con., Book ii. 7, § 102.
‖ Dig., vol. ii., p. 183.

what has been stated by Mr. Colebrooke in his Treatise on Obligations and Contracts, that though by the Hindu law, all things done by force are pronounced null, yet in fact they are, in every system of jurisprudence, *voidable* rather than *void*; as they are susceptible of confirmation by assent subsequent, whether express or tacit.*

Under the head of fraud, it may be observed, that any fraudulent practice (to which the word in the original, *Chhala*, is synonymous), vitiates a contract;† and in a contract of sale, if the vendor, having shown a specimen of property free from blemish, deliver blemished property, the vendee may return it at any time and the vendor is liable to pay a fine and damages, on account of his dishonesty.‡

Of incompetency to contract, where the possession and even the proprietary right exists, there are frequent instances. The most familiar is that of a coparcener, who is prohibited from giving, mortgaging, or selling his own share of the immoveable estate, except at a time of distress for the support of his household.§ According to the law, however, as current in Bengal the contract, though not valid so far as regards the shares of the other parceners, is valid so far as regards the seller's own share.|| And not only are the survivors answerable for a debt contracted by their deceased partner, if the sum borrowed was applied to

* Chap. vii., § 109.
† Ibid.
‡ *Katyáyana* and *Nárada*, cited in Dig., vol. ii., pp. 323, 325.
§ *Vyása*, cited in Dig., vol. iii., p. 433.
|| Ibid, p. 434.

their use; but, according to *Manu*, "should even a slave make a contract in the name of his absent master for the behoof of the family, that master, whether in his own country or abroad, shall not rescind it." A similar prohibition extends to the case of widows on whom the property of their husbands has devolved, and who are declared incompetent to alienate, except for special purposes; and in a case recently adjudicated, where the heirs of a person deceased refused payment of a bond contracted by his widow (also dead), and in which it was proved that part of the amount was expended in payment of her husband's debts, it was held, that the heirs were liable for so much of the amount as had been so laid out, but that the widow could not saddle the estate or the heirs with any unnecessary burthen;* and it has been laid down as a general principle by Mr. Colebrooke, that the head of a family is answerable for necessaries supplied for the indispensable use of it, and for the subsistence of the persons whom he is bound to maintain, whether it be his wife, his parent, his child, his slave, his servant, his pupil, or his apprentice to whom the necessaries are furnished, and goods indispensably requisite are delivered.†

In recapitulating the causes of incapacity, *Yájnyawalkya* observes: "A contract made by a person intoxicated or insane, or grievously disordered or disabled, by an infant, or a man agitated by fear or the like, or in the name of another by a person without authority,

* *Vyása* cited in Dig., vol. iii., p. 201. † Obl. and Con., Book ii., § 49.

is utterly null." Upon the above passage *Jagannátha* comments: "Singly the gift of wages of a man possessing his senses is valid; joined with madness or the like, the intentional payment of wages during a lucid interval may also be valid; but singly a gift by a man affected by insanity or the like is void." From this comment the principle may be deduced that the act of a lunatic may be effectual, if the contract be not onerous and the agreement rational, on the presumption of the act having been done during a lucid interval; but that where it may be prejudicial to him, and unattended with any benefit, it should be held to be *ipso facto* void: so also the validity of a deed executed by a man in his last illness should be upheld, if it be proved that he was of sound mind at the time of its execution; but otherwise, if it appeared that his mind was not in its natural state.

This point was ruled by the Sadr Diwání Adálat in a suit by a Hindu widow against the brothers of her husband, who died childless, to which the defendants pleaded a conveyance from the brother to them, executed during mortal sickness, four days before he died; and it was held, that in law, the only question was, whether in point of fact he was of sound mind at the time.*

Eight gifts, according to *Katyáyana*, are not subject to revocation or retraction: what has been given as wages, as the price of an entertainment, as the price

* Case of Radhamaní Dibia *v.* Shamchandra and Rúdrachandra, S.D.A. Reports, vol. i., p. 85.

of goods sold, as a nuptial gift to a bride or her family, as an acknowledgement to a benefactor, as a present to a worthy man, from natural affection, or from friendship.* *Harita* declares: "A promise *legally* made in words, but not performed in deed, is a debt of conscience, both in this world and in the next; but where a promise has been made, or a thing given, to a person whom the law declares incapable of receiving, or where it has been given for a consideration unperformed, the law permits the nonperformance of the promise in the one case, and the revocation in the other.† It is a general rule, that in the case of a pledge, a gift, or a sale, the prior contract has the greatest force, and that in all other contested matters the latest act should prevail.‡

The liquidation of debts is rigorously enjoined: for instance, it is provided that sons must pay the debt of their father, when proved, as if it were their own, that is, with interest, and whether they have inherited assets or not. The son's son must pay the debt of his grandfather, but without interest; and his son, that is, the great-grandson, shall not be compelled to discharge the debt, unless he be heir and have assets.§ The reason of this last-mentioned distinction is not very obvious, nor does it appear why the equitable principle of rendering assets requisite to responsibility

* Dig., vol. ii., p. 174. † Dig., vol. ii., p. 171.

‡ *Yájnyawalkya*, cited in Dig., vol. ii., p. 477.

§ Dig., vol. i., p. 266. According to Sir William Jones, where there are no assets, the son and grandson are under a moral and religious, but not a civil, obligation to pay the debts. See note to ibid.

should be limited to the great-grandson alone. But in all cases, the liability extends only to just and reasonable debts. Hindu gifts are not binding on representatives; and in a case where a person contracted to pay to another a sum of money in consideration of that person's giving his daughter in marriage to the son of the contracting party, it was held that the contract was not binding after his death; the law not permitting money to be given for a bride, and the consideration consequently not being a legal one:* and it should be observed, that in all such cases the turpitude is considered to be on the side of the receiver, the giver not being deemed to have seriously intended to give.†

I deem it wholly superfluous to enter into further disquisition relative to the law of contracts, bailment, or other matters connected with judicial proceedings. They who are desirous of further information, and other miscellaneous matters, should consult the "Elements of Hindu Law," which contains an epitome of the law of contracts, and "Considerations on the Hindu Law, as current in Bengal," in which will be found a compilation of the principal rules connected with the subject. Were any outline of the subjects alluded to attempted in this place, the result would probably be a repetition, in substance, of what has been laid down by the above-mentioned authorities. The rules connected with the law of evidence are few and simple. The testimony of any person interested in the case is

* Bom. Rep., vol. ii., p. 194.

† Obl. and Con., Book ii., § 124.

not admissible. Various descriptions of incompetent witnesses are enumerated, and much is left to the discretion of the judge with respect to the credit which should be attached to testimony. In this last resort discovery may be had by compelling a defendant to make oath, or by ordeal. On the subject of evidence, it will be perceived, that one or two cases have been propounded to the Hindu law officers in the *mofussil* courts: but with reference to this and other topics connected with judicial proceedings generally, I beg to refer to the following chapters.*

* As already stated, the rules affecting evidence and the like, according to the Hindu laws, not regulating in any way the practice of the Courts in India, the chapters referred to, "although full of curious and interesting matter," have not been reprinted.—W.

PRINCIPLES

OF

MOHAMMADAN LAW.

PRELIMINARY REMARKS.

THE want of some practical information on the subject of Mohammadan Law has long been felt and acknowledged by those whose duty it is to decide matters of civil controversy agreeably to its principles. The translation of the *Hedaya,* indeed, is calculated to extend a general knowledge of that Code, but it is of little utility as a work of reference, to indicate the Law on any particular point which may be submitted to judicial decision. Questions which are likely to be litigated give place to extravagant hypotheses, the occurrence of real cases, similar to which, is beyond the verge of probability. The arrangement is immethodical; the most prolix and irrelevant discussions are introduced; every argument, however absurd, both for and against each particular tenet, is urged and combated (often with doubtful success;) and the reader is frequently at a loss to determine which opinion to adopt and which to reject.

"No branch of Jurisprudence is more important than the Law of Successions or Inheritance; as it constitutes that part of any national system of laws which is the most peculiar and distinct, and which is of most frequent use and extensive application."*

The subject unquestionably is of the greatest importance, as affecting the interests of all descriptions of people; but the *Hedaya* is entirely silent on the subject. It deserves special notice as giving rise to interminable litigation; a result attributable, more probably, to the almost universal ignorance of the people who are affected by it, than to any intricacy or obscurity of the Law itself. No English writer, that I am aware of, has treated of the Mohammadan Law of Inheritance excepting Sir William Jones, who translated the *Sirajiya*, a celebrated work on that subject; but, being a version of a scientific Arabic treatise, the style of his work is necessarily abstruse, so much so, that a knowledge of the original language is almost requisite to the study of the translation. In his abstract translation of its commentary (the *Sharafiya*) he has introduced such illustrations only as

* Colebrooke's Preface to the two Treatises on the Hindu Law of Inheritance.

appeared to him (who was thoroughly acquainted with the text) necessary to facilitate the understanding of it. From these considerations I was induced to undertake the work which is now with diffidence submitted to the public. Conscious of my inability to do justice to the task, I may yet venture to express a hope, that my labours may prove of some assistance to my judicial brethren, or that, at least an abler individual may follow up with success the work which I have so imperfectly commenced. I am aware that, among other faults, I may be charged with being obscure, where I laboured at brevity, and with being tiresome, where my object was illustration. I can only say that I have endeavoured, as much as was in my power, to avoid technicalities, and to treat the subject with all the perspicuity of which it is susceptible. I have spared myself no pains in my researches to establish the accuracy of the legal doctrines here laid down, and to those who are disposed to view with approbation any attempt, however humble, at the promotion of justice, it may perhaps seem reasonable, that the disadvantages of the author should be weighed against his imperfections. Continual want of leisure and occasional privation of health have attended me during the progress of this work. I should mention, that the compilation is (excepting the assistance derived from learned natives) entirely and exclusively my own, and that it consequently possesses no official weight whatever, and no authority, beyond that which may be ascribed to it by individual confidence.*

W. H. MACNAGHTEN.

* The original continues the introduction with an interesting and learned series of remarks upon the laws of the Mohammadans especially in relation to those of other nations; for these remarks the entire work must be referred to, as their insertion would have been foreign to the object of this edition.

H. H. W.

PRINCIPLES

OF

MOHAMMADAN LAW.

CHAPTER I.

PRINCIPLES OF INHERITANCE.

SECTION I.

GENERAL RULES.

1. There is no distinction between real and personal, nor between ancestral and acquired property, in the Mohammadan Law of Inheritance.

2. Primogeniture confers no superior right. All the sons, whatever their number, inherit equally.

3. The share of a daughter is half the share of a son, whenever they inherit together.

4. A will made in favour of one son, or of one heir, cannot take effect to the prejudice and without the consent of the other sons, or the other heirs.

5. Debts are claimable before legacies, and legacies

(which however cannot exceed one-third of the testator's estate, must be paid before the inheritance is distributed.

6. Slavery, homicide, difference of religion and difference of allegiance, exclude from inheritance.

7. But persons not professing the Mohammadan faith may be heirs to those of their own persuasion: in the case of persons who are of the Mohammadan faith, difference of allegiance does not exclude from inheritance.

8. To the estate of a deceased person, a plurality of persons having different relations to the deceased, may succeed simultaneously, according to their respectively allotted shares, and inheritance may partly ascend lineally, and partly descend lineally at the same time.

9. The son of a person deceased shall not represent such person if he died before his father. He shall not stand in the same place as the deceased would have done had he been living, but shall be excluded from the inheritance, if he have a paternal uncle. For instance, A, B, and C are grandfather, father, and son. The father B dies in the lifetime of the grandfather A. In this case the son C shall not take *jure repraesentationis*, but the estate will go to the other sons of A.

10. Sons, son's sons and their lineal descendants, in how low a degree soever, have no specific share assigned to them: the general rule is that they take all the property after the legal sharers are satisfied, unless there are daughters; in which case each daughter takes a share equal to half of what is taken by each son. For instance, where there are a father, a mother, a husband, a wife, and daughters, but little remains as the portion of sons; but

where there are no legal sharers nor daughters, the sons take the whole property.

11. Parents, children, husband and wife must, in all cases, get shares, whatever may be the number or degree of the other heirs.

12. It is a general rule that a brother shall take double the share of a sister. The exception to it is in the case of brothers and sisters by the same mother only, but by different fathers.

13. The portions of those who are legal sharers only, and not residuary heirs, can be stated determinately, but the portions receivable by those who are both sharers and residuaries cannot be stated generally, and must be adjusted with reference to each particular case. For instance, in the case of a husband and wife, who are sharers only, their portion of inheritance is fixed for all cases that can occur; but in the case of daughters and sisters who are, under some circumstances, legal sharers, and under others residuaries, and in the case of fathers and grandfathers who are, under some circumstances, legal sharers only, and under others, residuaries also, the extent of their portions depends entirely upon the degree of relation of the other heirs and their number.*

* Daughters without sons are legal sharers, and so are sisters without brothers, but with them they become merely residuaries. Grandfathers and fathers with sons, son's sons, etc., are legal sharers, but with daughters only they are residuaries, as well as legal sharers.

SECTION II.

OF SHARERS AND RESIDUARIES.

14. The widow takes an eighth of her husband's estate where there are children or son's children, how low soever, and a fourth where there are none.

15. The husband takes a fourth of his wife's estate where there are children or son's children, how low soever, and a moiety where there are none.

16. Where there is no son and there is only one daughter, she takes a moiety of the property as her legal share.

17. Where there is no son, and there are two or more daughters, they take two-thirds of the property as their legal share.

18. Where there is no son, nor daughter, nor son's son, the son's daughters take as the daughters, namely, a moiety is the legal share of one and two-thirds of two or more.

19. Where there is one daughter, the son's daughters take a sixth, but where there are two or more daughters they take nothing.

20. Where there is a son's son, however, or a son's grandson, the son's daughters take a share equal to half of what is allotted to the grandson or great-grandson.

21. Brothers and sisters can never take any share of the property, where there is a son or son's son, how low soever, or a father or grandfather.*

* It is the orthodox opinion that the grandfather excludes brethren of the whole blood and those by the same father only. Among the Shias, who

22. Where there are uterine brothers, the sisters take a share equal to half of what is taken by the brothers; and they being then residuaries, the amount of their shares varies according to circumstances.

23. In default of sons, son's sons, daughters and son's daughters, where there is only one sister and no uterine brother, she takes a moiety of the property.

24. In default of sons, son's sons, daughters and son's daughters, where there are two or more sisters and no uterine brother, they take two-thirds of the property.

25. Where there are daughters or son's daughters and no brothers, the sisters take what remains after the daughters or son's daughters have realized their shares; such residue being half, should there be only one daughter or son's daughter, and one-third should there be two or more.

26. A distinction is made between the two descriptions of half brothers and half sisters. Half brothers and half sisters, who are by the same father only, can never inherit a half brother's estate while there are both brothers and sisters by the same father and mother, but those by the same mother only do inherit with brethren of the whole blood.

27. Where there is only one sister by the same father and mother, the half sisters by the same father only,

adhere to the doctrine of the two disciples, the contrary opinion is maintained. The terms "grandfather" and "grandmother" are intended to include all ancestors, in whatever degree of ascent, between whom and the deceased no female intervenes.

supposing them to have no uterine brother, take one-sixth as their legal shares.

28. Where there are two or more sisters by the same father and mother, the half sisters by the same father only, supposing them to have no uterine brother, take nothing.

29. Where, however, the half sisters by the same father only, have an uterine brother, they each take a share equal to half of what is allotted to him.

30. Among brothers and sisters by the same mother only, difference of sex makes no distinction in the amount of the shares, contrary to the case of brothers and sisters by the same father and mother, and brothers and sisters by the same father only; but the general rule of a double share to the male applies to their issue.

31. Where there is one brother by the same mother only, or one sister by the same mother only, his or her share is one-sixth provided there are no children of the deceased nor son's children, nor father, nor grandfather, and where there are two or more children by the same mother only, their share is one-third.

32. Where there is a son of the deceased, or son's son, how low soever, or two or more brothers and sisters, the father will take one-sixth.

33. Where there are children, or son's children, how low soever, or two or more brothers and sisters, the mother will take one-sixth.

34. Where there are no children, nor son's children, and only one brother or sister, the mother will take one-third with a widow or widower, if she have a grandfather

to share with, instead of a father; but a third of the remainder only, after the shares of the widow or widower have been satisfied, if there be a father to share with her.

35. Grandfathers can never take any share of the property where there is a father.

36. Where there is a son of the deceased or son's son, how low soever, and no father, the grandfather will take one-sixth.

37. Grandmothers can never take any share of the property where there is a mother, nor can paternal grandmothers inherit where there is a father.

38. Paternal female ancestors of whatever degree of ascent are also excluded by the grandfather, except the father's mother; she not being related through the grandfather.

39. The share of a maternal grandmother is one-sixth, and the same share belongs to the paternal grandmother where there is no father.

40. Two or three grandmothers being of equal degree take the sixth equally.

41. But grandmothers who are nearer in degree to the deceased, exclude those who are more distant.

42. A maternal grandfather and the mother of a maternal grandfather are not entitled to any specific share, they being termed false ancestors, and not included in the number of sharers or residuaries.

SECTION III.

OF DISTANT KINDRED.

43. Where there is no son nor daughter, nor son's son, nor son's daughter however low in descent, nor father, nor grandfather, nor other lineal male ancestor, nor mother, nor mother's mother, nor father's mother, nor other lineal female ancestor, nor widow, nor husband, nor brother of the half or whole blood; nor sons, how low soever, of the brethren of the whole blood or of those by the same father only, nor sister of the half or whole blood, nor paternal uncle, nor paternal uncle's son, how low soever (all of whom are termed either sharers or residuaries),* the daughter's children and the children of the son's daughters succeed; and they are termed the first class of distant kindred.

44. In default of all those above enumerated, the grandfathers and grandmothers of that description, who are neither sharers nor residuaries, succeed; and they are termed the second class of distant kindred.

45. In their default the sister's children, and the brother's daughters, and the sons of the brothers by

* Of the persons here enumerated the following males are legal sharers, namely, the father, the grandfather or other lineal male ancestor, the husband and the brother of the half blood by the same mother only, and the following females, namely, the daughter, the son's daughter, the widow, the mother, the grandmother, the sister by the same father and mother, the sister by the same father only and the sister by the same mother only. The shares of these persons vary according to circumstances, and in particular instances some of them (as has been shown) are liable to exclusion altogether. The rest of the persons enumerated are residuaries only, and have no specific shares.

the same mother only, succeed; and they are termed the third class of distant kindred.

46. In their default the paternal aunts and uncles by the same mother only, and maternal uncles and aunts succeed; and they are termed the fourth class of distant kindred.

47. In their default the cousins, that is, the children of paternal aunts and uncles by the same mother only, and of maternal uncles and aunts succeed.

48. There is an exception to the above general rules, relative to the succession of distant kindred after residuaries. If the estate to be inherited belonged to an enfranchised slave, his manumittor and the heirs of such manumittor inherit, in preference to the distant kindred of the deceased.

49. The rule with regard to the succession of distant kindred is, that they take according to proximity of degree, and when equal, those who claim through one heir have a preference to those who claim through one not being an heir. For instance, the daughter of a son's daughter and the son of a daughter's daughter are equidistant in degree from the ancestor: but the former shall be preferred, by reason of the son's daughter being an heir, and the daughter's daughter not being an heir: if there should be a number of these descendants of equal degree, and all on the same footing with respect to the persons through whom they claim, but where the sexes of the ancestors differ in any stage of the ascent, the distribution will be made with reference to such difference of sex; regard being had to the stage at which the

difference first appeared: for instance, the two daughters of the daughter of a daughter's son will get twice as much as the two sons of a daughter's daughter's daughter; because one of the ancestors of the former was a male, whose portion is double that of a female.*

50. The succession also, with regard to the second class of distant kindred, is regulated nearly in the same manner, by proximity, and by the condition and sex of the person through whom the succession is claimed when the claimants are related on the same side: when the sides of relation differ, two-thirds go to the paternal, and one to the maternal side, without regard to the sex of the claimants.†

51. The same rules apply with regard to the third as to the first class of distant kindred; for instance, the brother's son's daughter and the sister's daughter's son are equidistant from the ancestor; but the former shall be preferred by reason of the brother's son being a residuary heir, and where they are equal in this respect the rule laid down for the first class is applicable to this.

* The opinion of Abú Yúsaf is that where the claimants are on the same footing with respect to the persons through whom they claim, regard should be had to the sexes of the claimants, and not to the sexes of their ancestors. But this, although the most simple, is not the most approved rule.

† The rule may be thus exemplified. The claimants being a maternal grandfather and the mother of a maternal grandfather, the former being more proximate excludes the latter; but suppose them to be the father of a maternal grandfather and the mother of a maternal grandfather: here the claimants are equal in point of proximity; the side of their relation is the same and they are equal with respect to the sex of the person through whom they claim, and in this case the only method of making the distribution is by having regard to the sexes of the claimants and by giving a double share to the male.

52. With regard to the fourth class all that need be said is, that (the sides of relation being equal) uncles and aunts of the whole blood are preferred to those of the half, and those who are connected by the same father only, to those by the same mother only. Where the strength of relation is also equal, as, for instance, where the claimants are a maternal uncle and a maternal aunt, of the whole blood, then the rule is, that the male shall have a share double that of the female. Where, however, one claimant is related through the father only, and the other is related through the mother only, the claimant related through the father shall exclude the other if the sides of their relation are the same; for instance, a maternal aunt by the same father only, will exclude a maternal aunt by the same mother only; but if the sides of their relation differ—for instance, if one of the claimants be a paternal aunt by the same father and mother, and the other be a maternal aunt by the same father only, no exclusive preference is given to the former, though she obtains two shares in virtue of her paternal relation.

53. The succession of the children of the above class, that is, the cousins, is regulated by the following rules: propinquity to the ancestor is the first rule. Where that is equal, the claimant through an heir inherits before the claimant through one not being an heir, without respect to the sex of the claimants; for instance, the daughter of a paternal uncle succeeds in preference to the son of a paternal aunt—unless the aunt is related on both the father's and mother's sides, and the relation of the uncle be by the same mother only. But where the son of a paternal aunt

by the same father and mother, and the son of a maternal aunt by the same father and mother, or by the same father only, claim together, the latter will not be excluded by the former; the only difference is, that two-thirds are the right of the claimant on the paternal side, and one-third that of the claimant on the mother's side. Should there be no difference between the strength of relation, the sides or the sexes of the persons through whom they claim, regard must be had to the sexes of the claimants themselves.

54. In the distribution among the descendants of this class, the same rule is applicable as to the descendants of the first class; for instance, the two daughters of the daughter of a paternal uncle's son will get twice as much as the two sons of the daughter of a paternal uncle's daughter, supposing the relation of the uncles to be the same, and in case of equality in all other respects regard must be had as above, to the sexes of the claimants.*

55. In default of distant kindred, he has a right to

* In considering the doctrine of succession of distant kindred attention must be paid to the following points. First, their relative distance in degree of relation from the deceased, whether a greater or lesser number of degrees removed. Secondly, it must be ascertained whether any of the claimants are the children of heirs. If so, preference must be shown to such children. Thirdly, their strength of relation, whether they are of the half or whole blood. Fourthly, their sides of relation, whether connected by the father's or mother's side; and Fifthly, the sexes of the persons through whom they claim, whether male or female. With respect to this latter point, however, a difference of opinion exists; it being maintained by some authorities that *cæteris paribus* no regard should be had to the mere sex of the person through whom the claim is made, but that the adjustment should be made according to the sex of the claimants themselves. But the contrary is the most approved doctrine. It should be recollected too, that whenever the sides of relation differ, those connected through the father are entitled to twice as much as those connected through the mother, whatever may be the sexes of the claimants.

succeed whom the deceased ancestor acknowledged conditionally, or unconditionally, as his kinsman: provided the acknowledgment was never retracted, and provided it cannot be established that the person in whose favour the acknowledgment was made belongs to a different family.

56. In default of all these, there being no will, the property will escheat to the Public Treasury; but this only where no individual has the slightest claim.

SECTION IV.

PRIMARY RULES OF DISTRIBUTION.

57. Where there are two claimants, the share of one of whom is half, and of the other a fourth, the division must be made by four; as in the case of a husband and an only daughter, the property is made into four parts, of which the former takes one and the latter two. The remaining fourth will revert to the daughter.

58. Where there are two claimants, the share of one of whom is half, and of the other an eighth, the division must be made by eight; as in the case of a wife and a daughter, the property is made into eight parts, of which the daughter takes four and the wife one. The surplus three shares revert to the daughter.

59. No case can occur of two claimants, the one entitled to a fourth and the other to an eighth; nor of three claimants, the one entitled to half, the other to a fourth, and the third to an eighth.

60. Where there are two claimants, the share of one of whom is one-sixth, and of the other one-third; as in the case of a mother and father being the only claimants, the property is made into six parts, of which the mother takes two and the father one as his legal share. The surplus three shares revert to the father.

61. Where there are two claimants, the share of one of whom is one-sixth, and of the other two-thirds; as in the case of a father and two daughters being the only claimants, the property is made into six parts, of which the father takes one as his legal share, and the two daughters four. The surplus share reverts to the father.

62. Where there are two claimants, the share of one of whom is one-third, and of the other two-thirds; as in the case of a mother and two sisters, the property is made into three parts, of which the mother takes one and the two sisters two.

63. No case can occur of three claimants, the one entitled to one-sixth, the other to one-third, and the other to two-thirds.

64. Where a husband inherits from his childless wife (his share in this case being one half), and there are other claimants entitled to one-sixth, one-third, or two-thirds, such as a father, a mother, or two sisters, the division must be by six.

65. Where a husband inherits from his wife who leaves children, or a wife from her childless husband (the shares of these persons respectively in these cases being one-fourth), and there are other claimants entitled to one-sixth, one-third, or two-thirds, the division must be made by twelve.

66. Where a wife inherits from her husband, leaving children, her share in that case being one-eighth, and there are other claimants entitled to one-sixth, one-third, or two-thirds, the division must be made by twenty-four.

67. Where six is the number of shares into which it is proper to distribute the estate, but that number does not suit to satisfy all the sharers without a fraction, it may be increased to seven, eight, nine, or ten.

68. Where twelve is the number, and it does not suit, it may be increased to thirteen, fifteen, or seventeen.

69. Where twenty-four is the number and it does not suit, it may be increased to twenty seven.

SECTION V.

RULES OF DISTRIBUTION AMONG NUMEROUS CLAIMANTS.

70. Numbers are said to be *mutamásil*, or equal, where they exactly agree.

71. They are said to be *mutadákhil*, or concordant, where the one number being multiplied, exactly measures the other.

72. They are said to be *mutawáfik*, or composite, where a third number measures them both.

73. They are said to be *mutabayin*, or prime, where no third number measures them both.

74. There are seven rules of distribution, the first three of which depend upon a comparison between the number

of heirs and the number of the shares; and the four remaining ones upon a comparison of the numbers of the different sets of heirs, after a comparison of the number of each set of heirs with their respective shares.

75. The first is when, on a comparison of the number of heirs and the number of shares, it appears that they exactly agree, there is no occasion for any arithmetical process. Thus, where the heirs are a father, a mother, and two daughters, the share of the parents is one-sixth each, and that of the daughters two-thirds. Here according to principle 61, the division must be by six, of which each parent takes one, and the remaining four go to the two daughters.

76. The second is when, on a comparison of the number of heirs and the number of shares, it appears that the heirs cannot get their portions without a fraction, and that some third number measures them both, when they are termed *mutawáfik*, or composite; as in the case of a father, a mother and ten daughters. Here, according to principle 61, the division must be by six. But when each parent has taken a sixth, there remain only four to be distributed among the ten daughters, which cannot be done without a fraction, and on a comparison of the number of heirs who cannot get their portions without a fraction, and the number of shares remaining for them, they appear to be composite, or agree in two. In this case the rule is, that half the number of such heirs, which is five, must be multiplied into the number of the original division 6: thus $5 \times 6 = 30$; of which the parents take ten, or five each, and the daughters twenty, or two each.

77. The third is when, on a comparison of the number of the heirs and the number of shares, it appears that the heirs cannot get their portions without a fraction, and that there is one over and above between the number of shares remaining for them. This is termed *mutabayin*, or prime, as in the case of a father, a mother, and five daughters. Here also, according to principle 61 above quoted, the division must be by six. But when each parent has taken a sixth, there remain only four to be distributed among the five daughters, which cannot be done without a fraction, and on a comparison of the number of heirs who cannot get their portions without a fraction and the number of shares remaining for them, they appear to be *mutabayin*, or prime. In this case the rule is, that the whole number of such heirs, which is five, must be multiplied into the number of the original division. Thus $5 \times 6 = 30$; of which the parents take ten, or five each, and the daughters twenty, or four each.

78. The fourth is when, on a comparison of the different sets of heirs, it appears that one or more sets cannot get their portions without a fraction and that all the sets are *mutamásil*, or equal, as in the case of six daughters, three grandmothers, and three paternal uncles; in which case, according to principle 61, the division must be by six. Here, in the first instance, a comparison must be made between the several sets and their respective shares. The share of the daughters is two-thirds, but two-thirds of six is four, and four compared with the number of daughters six, is *mutawáfik*, or composite, agreeing in two. The share of the three grandmothers is one-sixth, but one-sixth of six

is one, and one compared with the number of grandmothers is *mutabayin*, or prime. The remaining share, which is one, will devolve on the three paternal uncles; but one compared with three is also *mutabayin*, or prime.

Then the rule is, that the sets of heirs themselves must be compared with each other, by the whole where it appears that they were *mutadákhil*, or concordant; or *mutabayin*, or prime; and by the measure where it appears that they were *mutawáfik*, or composite, and if agreeing in two, by half. In the instance of the daughters, the result of the former comparison was, that they agreed in two; consequently the half of their number must be compared with the whole number of the grandmothers and of the uncles, in whose cases the comparison showed a prime result. Thus $3 = 3$ and $3 = 3$, which being *mutamásil*, or equal, the rule is, that one of the numbers be multiplied into the number of the original division. Thus $3 \times 6 = 18$; of which the daughters will take (two-thirds) twelve, or two each; the grandmothers will take (a sixth) three, or one each; and the paternal uncles will take the remaining three, or one each.

79. The fifth is when, on a comparison of the different sets of heirs, it appears that one or more sets cannot get their portions without a fraction, and that the sets are *mutadákhil*, or concordant; as in the case of four wives, three grandmothers, and twelve paternal uncles. In this case, according to principle 65, the division must be by twelve.

Here, in the first instance, a comparison must be made between the several sets and their respective shares. Thus the share of the four wives is one-fourth; but the fourth of twelve is three, and three compared with the number of wives is *mutabayin*, or prime. The share of the three grandmothers is one-sixth; but the sixth of twelve is two, and two compared with the number of grandmothers is also prime. The remaining shares, which are seven, will devolve on the twelve paternal uncles; but seven compared with twelve is also prime.

Then the rule is, that the sets of heirs themselves must be compared, the whole of each with the whole of each, as the preceding results show that they are prime, on the comparison of the several heirs with their respective shares. Thus $4 \times 3 = 12$, and $3 \times 4 = 12$, which being concordant, the one number measuring the other exactly, the rule is, that the greater number must be multiplied into the number of the original division. Thus $12 \times 12 = 144$; of which the wives will get (one-fourth) thirty-six, or nine each; the grandmothers (one-sixth) twenty-four, or eight each; and the paternal uncles the remaining eighty-four, or seven each.

80. The sixth is when, on a comparison of the different sets of heirs, it appears that one or more sets cannot get their portions without a fraction, and that some of the sets are *mutawáfik*, or composite, with each other: as in the case of four wives, eighteen daughters, fifteen female ancestors, and six paternal uncles: in which case, according to principle 66, the original division must be by twenty-four. Here, in the first place, a comparison must be made between the several sets and their respective shares. Thus the share of the four wives is an eighth; but an eighth of twenty-four is three, and three compared with the number

of wives is *mutabayin*, or prime. The shares of the eighteen daughters is two-thirds; but two-thirds of twenty-four is sixteen, and sixteen compared with the number of daughters eighteen, is composite, and they agree in two. The share of the fifteen female ancestors is one-sixth; but a sixth of twenty-four is four, and four compared with the number of female ancestors, fifteen, is prime. The remaining share, which is one, will devolve on the six paternal uncles as residuaries; but one and six are prime.

Then the rule is, that the sets of heirs themselves must be compared; by the whole where the preceding result shows that they were prime, and by their measure where it shows that they were composite. Thus $4 \times 2 = 9 - 1$, which being prime, the one number must be multiplied by the other. This result must then be compared with the whole of the third set; because the preceding result shows that set to have been prime. Thus $15 \times 2 = 36 - 6$ and $6 = 15 - 9$ and $6 = 9 - 3$, which agreeing in three, the third of one number, must be multiplied into the whole of the other. This result must also be compared with the whole of the fourth set; because the preceding result shows that set to have been prime. Thus $6 \times 30 = 180$, which being concordant or agreeing in six, the sixth of one number must be multiplied into the whole of the other; but as it is obvious that by this process the result would still be the same, multiplication is needless. Then this result must be multiplied into the number of the original division. Thus $180 \times 24 = 4320$; of which the four wives will get an eighth, five hundred and forty, or one hundred and thirty-five each; the eighteen daughters two-thirds, two thousand eight hundred and eighty, or one hundred and sixty each; the female ancestors one-sixth, seven hundred and twenty, or forty-eight each; and the paternal uncles the remaining one hundred and eighty, or thirty each.

81. The seventh and last is when, on a comparison of the different sets of heirs, it appears that all the sets are *mutabayin*, or prime, and no one of them agrees with the other; as in the case of two wives, six female ancestors, ten daughters, and seven paternal uncles. Here, according to principle 66, the original division must be by twenty-four.

In the first instance, a comparison must be made between the several sets of heirs and their respective shares. Thus the share of the two wives is one-eighth; but the eighth of twenty-four is three, and three compared with the number of wives is prime. The share of the six female ancestors is one-sixth; but the sixth of twenty-four is four, and four compared with the number of female ancestors is composite, or agrees in two. The share of the ten daughters is two-thirds, and two-thirds of twenty-four is sixteen, and sixteen compared with the number of daughters is also composite or agrees in two. The remaining share, which is one, will devolve on the seven paternal uncles; but one and seven are prime.

Then the rule is, that the sets of heirs themselves must be compared; by the whole where the preceding result shows that they were prime, and by the half or other measure, where it shows that they were composite. Agreeably to this rule the whole of the first set of heirs must be compared with half the second: thus $2 = 3 - 1$, which numbers being prime must be multiplied into each other. Then the result must be compared with the half of the next set, the former result having here also agreed in two. Thus $5 = 6 - 1$, which being prime, must be multiplied into each other. Then the result must be compared with the whole of the next set, the former result here having been prime. Thus $7 \times 4 = 30 - 2$ and $2 \times 3 = 7 - 1$, which being also prime, must be multiplied into each other. Thus $30 \times 7 = 210$, in which case the rule is, that this last product must be multiplied into the number of the original division. Thus $210 \times 24 = 5040$; of which the wives will take an eighth, six hundred and thirty, or three hundred and fifteen each; the female ancestors a sixth, eight hundred and forty, or one hundred and forty each; the daughters two-thirds, three thousand three hundred and sixty, or three hundred and thirty-six each; and the paternal uncles the remaining two hundred and ten, or thirty each.

82. When the whole number of shares into which an estate should be made, has been found, the mode of ascertaining the number of portions to which each set of heirs is entitled, is to multiply the portions originally assigned them, by the same number by which the aggregate of the original portions was multiplied; as an easy example of which rule the following case may be mentioned. There are a widow, eight daughters, and four paternal uncles; the shares of the two first sets being one-eighth and two-thirds, the estate, according to principle 66, must be made originally into twenty-four parts, of which the widow is entitled to three, the daughters to sixteen, and there remain five to be divided among the four paternal uncles,

but which cannot be done without a fraction. Here the proportion between the shares and the heirs who cannot get their portions without a fraction, must be ascertained, and $4 = 5 - 1$ being prime, the rule is (see No. 77), to multiply the number of the original division by the whole number of heirs so situated. Thus $24 \times 4 = 96$. Here, to find the shares of each set, multiply what each was originally declared entitled to, by the number by which the aggregate of all the original portions was multiplied. Thus $3 \times 4 = 12$, the share of the widow; $16 \times 4 = 64$, the share of the daughters; and $5 \times 4 = 20$, the share of the paternal uncles.

83. To find the portion of each individual in the several sets of heirs, ascertain how many times the number of persons in each set may be multiplied into the number of shares ultimately assigned to each set. Thus $8 \times 8 = 64$, and $5 \times 4 = 20$. Here eight will be the share of each daughter, and four the share of each paternal uncle, which, with the twelve which formed the share of the widow, will make up the required number ninety-six.

SECTION VI.

OF THE EXCLUSION FROM AND PARTIAL SURRENDER OF INHERITANCE.

84. Exclusion is either entire or partial. By entire exclusion is meant, the total privation of right to inherit. By partial exclusion is meant, a diminution of the portion to which the heir would otherwise be entitled. Entire

exclusion is brought about by some of the personal disqualifications enumerated in principle (6), or by the intervention of an heir, in default of whom a claimant would have been entitled to take, but by reason of whose intervention he has no right of inheritance.

85. Those who are entirely excluded by reason of personal disqualification, do not exclude other heirs either entirely or partially; but those who are excluded by reason of some intervening heir, do, in some instances, partially exclude others.

86. For instance, a man dies, leaving a father, a mother, and two sisters, who are infidels. Here the mother will get her third, notwithstanding the existence of the two infidel sisters, who are excluded by reason of their personal disqualification; but had they not been infidels, she would only have been entitled to a sixth, although the sisters, who partially exclude her, are themselves entirely excluded by reason of the intervention of the father.

87. If one of the heirs choose to surrender his portion of the inheritance for a consideration, still he must be included in the division. Thus in the case of there being a husband, a mother, and a paternal uncle, the shares are one-half and one-third. Here, according to principle 64, the property must be made into six shares; of which the husband was entitled to three, the mother to two, and the paternal uncle, as a residuary, to the remaining one. Now supposing the estate left to amount to six lacks of rupees, and the husband to content himself with two, still, as far as affects the mother, the division must be made as if he had been a party, and of the remaining four lacks the

mother must get two; otherwise, were he not made a party, the mother would get only one-third of four, instead of one-third of six lacks as her legal share, and the remainder would go to the uncle as residuary.

SECTION VII.

OF THE INCREASE.

88. The increase is where there are a certain number of legal sharers, each of whom is entitled to a specific portion, and it is found, on a distribution of the shares into which it is necessary to make the estate, that there is not a sufficient number to satisfy the just demands of all the claimants.

89. It takes effect in three cases; either when the estate should be made into six shares, or when it should be made into twelve, or when it should be made into twenty-four. See principles (67, 68, 69). One example will suffice.

90. A woman leaves a husband, a daughter, and both parents. Here the property should be made into twelve parts, of which, after the husband has taken his fourth or three, and the parents have taken their two-sixths or four, there remain only five shares for the daughter instead of six, or the moiety to which by law she is entitled. In this case the number twelve, into which it was necessary to make the estate, must be increased to thirteen, with a view of enabling the daughter to realize six shares of the property.

SECTION VIII.

OF THE RETURN.

91. The return is where there being no residuaries, the surplus, after the distribution of the shares, returns to the sharers, and the doctrine of it is as follows:

92. It takes effect in four cases; first, where there is only one class of sharers unassociated with those not entitled to claim the return, as in the instance of two daughters or two sisters; in which case the surplus must be made into as many shares as there are sharers, and distributed among them equally.

93. Secondly, where there are two or more classes of sharers, unassociated with those not entitled to claim the return, as in the instance of a mother and two daughters; in which case the surplus must be made into as many shares as may correspond with the shares of inheritance to which the parties are entitled, and distributed accordingly. Thus the mother's share being one-sixth, and the two daughters' share two-thirds, the surplus must be made into six, of which the mother will take two and the daughters four.

94. Thirdly, when there is only one class of sharers, associated with those not entitled to claim to return, as in the instance of three daughters and a husband, in which case the whole estate must be divided into the smallest number of shares of which it is susceptible, consistently with giving the person excluded from the return his share of the inheritance (which is in this case four), and the husband will take one as his legal share or a fourth,

the remaining three going to the daughters as their legal shares and as the return; but if it cannot be so distributed without a fraction, as in the case of a husband and six daughters (three not being capable of division among six), the proportion must be ascertained between the shares and sharers. Thus $3 \times 2 = 6$, which agreeing in three, the rule is, that the number 4, into which the estate was intended to be distributed, must be multiplied by 2, that is, the measure or a third of the number of those entitled to the return. Thus $4 \times 2 = 8$, of which the husband will take two, and the daughters six, or one each; and if on a comparison as above, the result should be prime, as in the case of a husband and five daughters, the number 4, into which it was intended to distribute the estate, must be multiplied by 5, or the whole of the number of those entitled to a return. Thus $4 \times 5 = 20$, of which the husband will take five, and the daughters fifteen, or three each.

95. Fourthly, where there are two or more classes of sharers, associated with those not entitled to claim the return, as in the instance of a widow, four paternal grandmothers, and six sisters by the same mother only; in which case the whole estate must be divided into the smallest number of shares of which it was susceptible, consistently with giving the person excluded from the return her share of the inheritance (which is in this case four). Then after the widow has taken her share, there remain three to be divided among the grandmothers and half sisters; but the share of the grandmothers is one-sixth, and of the half sisters one-third, and here, to give

them their portions, the remainder should be made into six: but a third and a sixth of this number, amount to three, which agrees with the number to be divided among them; of which the half sisters will take two, and the grandmothers one. Had there been only one grandmother, and only two half sisters, there would have been no necessity for any further process, as the grandmother would have taken one-third, and the two half sisters the other two-thirds. But it is obvious, that two shares cannot be distributed among the six half sisters nor one among the four paternal grandmothers without a fraction. To find the number into which the remainder should be made, recourse must be had to the seventh principle of distribution. The proportion between the shares and the sharers respectively must first be ascertained. Thus $2 \times 3 = 6$, which being composite or agreeing in two, and $1 \times 3 = 4 - 1$, which being prime, the whole of one set of sharers must be compared with the half of the other. Thus $3 = 4 - 1$, which also being prime, one of the numbers must be multiplied by the other. Thus $3 \times 4 = 12$; and having found this number it must be multiplied into that of the original division. Thus $4 \times 12 = 48$, of which the grandmothers will get 12, or three each, 12 being to 48 as 1 to 4, and the half sisters 24, or 4 each, 24 being to 48 as 2 to 4, and the widow will take the remaining twelve. It is different if the shares of the persons entitled to a return do not agree with the number left for them, after deducting the share of the person not entitled to a return, as in the case of a widow, nine daughters and six paternal grandmothers. Here the property must in the first instance be made into eight shares, being the smallest number of which it is susceptible, consistently with giving the widow her share. Then, after the widow has taken her share, there remain seven to be divided among the daughters and the grandmothers; but the share of the grandmothers is one-sixth, and of the daughters two-thirds; and here to give them their portions the property divisible among them should be made into six parts; but a sixth and two-thirds of this number amount to five, which disagrees with the number to be divided among them; in which case the rule is, that the number of shares of those entitled to a return, must be multiplied by the number into which it was necessary to make the property originally. Thus $8 \times 5 = 40$, of which the widow will take five, the daughters will take twenty-eight, and the grandmothers seven. But it is obvious, that twenty-eight cannot be distributed among the nine daughters, nor seven among the six paternal grandmothers, without a fraction. To find the number into which the remainder should be distributed, recourse should be had to the sixth principle of distribution. The proportion between the shares and the sharers respectively must first be ascertained. Thus $9 \times 3 = 28 - 1$, and $6 = 7 - 1$, both of which being prime, the whole of one set of sharers must be compared with the whole of the other set. Thus $6 = 9 - 3$, which being concordant, or agreeing in three, the rule is that the third of one of the numbers must be multiplied into the whole of the other. Thus $3 \times 6 = 18$; and having found this number it must be multiplied into that of the preceding result. Thus $40 \times 18 = 720$, of which the daughters will get 504, or 56 each, 504 being to 720 as 28 to 40; the grandmothers will get 126, or 21 each, 126 being to 720 as 7 to 40; and the widow will get the remaining ninety.

SECTION IX.

OF VESTED INHERITANCES.

96. Where a person dies and leaves heirs, some of whom die prior to any distribution of the estate, the survivors are said to have vested interests in the inheritance; in which case the rule is, that the property of the first deceased must be apportioned among his several heirs living at the time of his death, and it must be supposed that they received their respective shares accordingly.

97. The same process must be observed with reference to the property of the second deceased, with this difference, that the proportion must be ascertained between the number of shares to which the second deceased was entitled at the first distribution, and the number into which it is requisite to distribute his estate to satisfy all the heirs.

98. If the proportion should appear to be prime, the rule is, that the aggregate and individual shares of the preceding distribution must be multiplied by the whole number of shares into which it is necessary to make the estate, at the subsequent distribution, and the individual shares at the subsequent distribution must be multiplied by the number of shares to which the deceased was entitled at the preceding one.

99. If the proportion should be concordant, or composite, the rule is, that the aggregate and individual shares

of the preceding distribution must be multiplied by the measure of the number of shares into which it is necessary to make the estate at the subsequent distribution; and the individual shares at the subsequent distribution must be multiplied by the measure of the number of shares to which the deceased was entitled at the preceding distribution.

100. For instance, a man dies leaving A, his wife, B and C, his two sons, and D and E, his two daughters; of whom A and D died before the distribution, the former leaving a mother, and the latter a husband.

At the first distribution the estate should be made into forty-eight shares, of which the widow will get six, the sons fourteen each, and the daughters seven each. On the death of the widow, leaving a mother and the above four children, her estate should, in the first instance, be made into thirty-six parts, of which the mother is entitled to six, the sons to ten each, and the daughters to five each; but being a case of vested inheritance, it becomes requisite to ascertain the proportion between the number of shares to which she was entitled at the preceding distribution, and the number into which it is necessary to make the estate. Thus $6 \times 6 = 36$, which proving concordant, or agreeing in six, the rule is, that the aggregate and individual shares of the preceding distribution be multiplied by six, or the measure of the number of shares into which it is necessary to make the estate at the second distribution. Thus $48 \times 6 = 288$, and $14 \times 6 = 84$ and $7 \times 6 = 42$; but the measure of the number to which the deceased was entitled at the preceding distribution being only one, it is needless to multiply by it the shares at the second distribution. On the death of one of the daughters, leaving her two brothers, her sister, and a husband, her estate should, in the first instance, be made into ten parts, of which her husband is entitled to five, her brothers to two each, and her sister to one; but being a case of vested inheritance, it becomes necessary to ascertain the proportion between the number of shares to which she was entitled at the preceding distribution, and the number into which it is necessary to make her estate. But she derived forty-seven shares from the preceding distributions (five at the second and forty-two at the first). Thus $10 \times 4 = 47 - 7$, and $7 = 10 - 3$, and $3 = 7 - 4$, and $3 = 4 - 1$, which proving prime or agreeing in a unit only, the rule is, that the aggregate and individual shares of the preceding distributions be multiplied by ten, or the whole number of shares into which it is necessary to make the estate at the third distribution. Thus $288 \times 10 = 2880$, and $84 \times 10 = 840$, and $42 \times 10 = 420$, and $6 \times 10 = 60$, and $10 \times 10 = 100$, and $5 \times 10 = 50$. Then the shares at the third distribution should be multiplied by the number of shares to which the deceased sister was entitled at the preceding distributions. Thus $5 \times 47 = 235$, and $2 \times 47 = 94$, and $1 \times 47 = 47$. Therefore of the 2880 shares, the son B will get $840 + 100 + 94 = 1034$; the son C $840 + 100 + 94 = 1034$; the daughter E $420 + 50 + 47 = 517$; the mother of A 60, and the husband of D 235.

SECTION X.

OF MISSING PERSONS AND POSTHUMOUS CHILDREN.

101. The property of a missing person is kept in abeyance for ninety years. His estate in this interval cannot derive any accession from the immediate death of others, nor can any person who dies during this interval inherit from him.

102. If a missing person be a coheir with others, the estate will be distributed as far as the others are concerned, provided they would take at all events, whether the missing person were living or dead. Thus in the case of a person dying, leaving two daughters, a missing son, and a son and daughter of such missing son. In this case the daughters will take half the estate immediately, as that must be their share at all events; but the grandchildren will not take any thing, as they are precluded on the supposition of their father being alive.

103. Where a person dies leaving his wife pregnant, and he has sons, the share of one son must be reserved in case a posthumous son should be born.

104. Where a person dies leaving his wife pregnant, and he has no sons, but there are other relatives who would succeed in the event only of his having no child (as would be the case, for instance, with a brother or sister), no immediate distribution of the property takes place.

105. But if those other relatives would succeed at

all events to some portion (larger without than with a child, as would be the case, for instance, with a mother), the property will be distributed, and the mother will obtain a sixth, the share to which she is necessarily entitled, and afterwards, if the child be not born alive, her portion will be augmented to one-third.

SECTION XI.

DE COMMORIENTIBUS.

106. Where two or more persons meet with a sudden death about the same time, and it is not known which died first, it will be presumed according to one opinion, that the youngest survived longest; but according to the more accurate and prevailing doctrine, it will be presumed that the death of the whole party was simultaneous, and the property left will be distributed among the surviving heirs, as if the intermediate heirs who died at the same time with the original proprietor had never existed.*

* The following case may be cited as an example of this rule. A, B and C are grandfather, father, and son. A and B perish at sea, without any particulars of their fate being known. In this case, if A have other sons, C will not inherit any of his property, because the law recognized no right by representation, and sons exclude grandsons. Mr. Christian in note to Blackstone's Commentaries (vol. ii., p. 516), notices a curious question that was agitated some time ago, where it was contended that when a parent and child perish together, and the priority of their deaths is unknown, it was a rule of the civil law to presume that the child survives the parent. He proceeds, however, to say, "But I should be inclined to think that our courts would require something more than presumptive evidence to support a claim of this nature." Some

SECTION XII.

OF THE DISTRIBUTION OF ASSETS.

107. What has preceded relates to the ascertainment of the shares to which the several heirs are *entitled;* but when the proper number of shares into which an estate should be made, may have been ascertained, it seldom happens that the assets of the estate exactly tally with such number; in other words, if it be found that the estate should be made into ten, or into fifty shares, it would seldom happen that the assets exactly amount in value to ten or fifty gold mohurs or rupees. To ascertain the proper shares of the different sets of heirs and creditors in such cases, the following rules are laid down:

108. When the number of shares has been found into which the estate should be divided, and the number of shares to which each set of heirs is entitled, the former number must be compared with the number of assets. If these numbers appear to be prime to each other, the rule is, that the share of each set of heirs must be multiplied into the number of assets, and the result divided by the number of shares into which it was found necessary to make the estate. For instance, a man dies, leaving a widow, two daughters and a paternal

curious cases *de commorientibus* may be seen in *Causes Célèbres*, vol. iii., 412 et seq., in one of which where a father and son were slain together in battle and on the same day the daughter became a professed nun, it was determined that her civil death was prior to the death of her father and brother, and that the brother having arrived at the age of puberty, should be presumed to have survived his father.

uncle, and property to the amount of 25 rupees. In this case, the estate should be originally divided into 24, of which the widow is entitled to 3, the daughters to 16, and the uncle to 5. Now to ascertain what shares of the estate left these heirs are entitled to, the above rule must be observed. Thus $3 \times 25 = 75$, and $16 \times 25 = 400$, and $5 \times 25 = 125$; but $75 \div 24 = 3\frac{3}{24}$, and $400 \div 24 = 16\frac{16}{24}$, and $125 \div 24 = 5\frac{5}{24}$.

109. If the numbers are composite, the rule is that the share of each set of heirs must be multiplied into the measure of the number of the assets, and the result divided by the measure of the number of shares into which it was found necessary to make the estate. For instance, a man dies, leaving the same number of heirs as above and property to the amount of fifty rupees. Now as 24 and 50 agree in 2 the measure of both numbers is half. Thus $3 \times 25 = 75$, and $16 \times 25 = 400$, and $5 \times 25 = 125$; but $75 \div 12 = 6\frac{3}{12}$, and $400 \div 12 = 33\frac{4}{12}$, and $125 \div 12 = 10\frac{5}{12}$.

110. If it be desired to ascertain the number of shares of the assets to which each individual heir is entitled, the same process must be resorted to, with this difference, that the number of assets must be compared with the share originally allotted to each individual heir, and the multiplication and division proceeded on as above. For instance, in the above case the original share of each daughter was 8, and $8 \times 25 = 200$, and $200 \div 12 = 16\frac{8}{12}$.

111. In a distribution of assets among creditors the rule is, that the aggregate sum of their debts must be

the number into which it is necessary to make the estate, and the sum of each creditor's claim must be considered as his share. For instance, supposing the debt of one creditor to amount to 16 rupees, of another to 5; and of another to 3, and the debtor to have left property to the amount of 21 rupees. By observing the same process as that laid down in principle (109), it will be found that the creditor to whom the debt of sixteen rupees was due, is entitled to 14 rupees, the creditor of 5 rupees to 4 rupees 6 annas, and the creditor of 3 rupees to 2 rupees 10 annas.

SECTION XIII.

OF PARTITION.

112. Where two persons claim partition of an estate which has devolved on them by inheritance, it should be granted; and so also where one heir claims it, provided the property admit of separation without detriment to its utility.

113. But where the property cannot be separated without detriment to its several parts, the consent of all the coheirs is requisite; so also where the estate consists of articles of different species.

114. On the occasion of a partition, the property (where it does not consist of money) should be distributed into several distinct shares, corresponding with the portions of the coheirs; each share should be appraised, and then recourse should be had to drawing of lots.

115. Another common mode of partition is by usufruct, where each heir enjoys the use or the profits of the property by rotation; but this method is subordinate to actual partition, and where one coheir demands separation, and the other a division of the usufruct only, the former claim is entitled to preference in all practicable cases.

CHAPTER II.

OF INHERITANCE ACCORDING TO THE IMAMIYA, OR SHIA DOCTRINE.

1. According to the tenets of this Sect, the right of inheritance proceeds from three different sources.

2. First, it accrues by virtue of consanguinity. Secondly, by virtue of marriage. Thirdly, by virtue of Willa.*

3. There are three degrees of heirs who succeed by virtue of consanguinity, and so long as there is any one of the first degree, even though a female, none of the second degree can inherit; and so long as there is any one of the second degree, none of the third can inherit.

4. The first degree comprises the parents, and the children, and grandchildren, how low in descent soever, the nearer of whom exclude the more distant. Both parents, or one of them inherit together with a child, a grandchild, or a great-grandchild; but a grandchild

* In a note to his translation of the Hedaya, Mr. Hamilton observes, that "there is no single word in our language fully expressive of this term. The shortest definition of it is, 'the relation between the master (or patron) and his Freedman,' but even this does not express the whole meaning." Had he proceeded to state "and the relation between two persons who had made a reciprocal testamentary contract," the definition might have been more complete.

does not inherit together with a child, nor a great-grandchild with a grandchild.

5. This degree is divided into two classes; the roots which are limited and the branches which are unlimited. The former are the parents who are not represented by their parents; the latter are the children who are represented by their children. An individual of one class does not exclude an individual of the other, though his relation to the deceased be more proximate; but the individuals of either class exclude each other in proportion to their proximity.

6. No claimant has a title to inherit with children, but the parents, or the husband and wife.

7. The children of sons take the portions of sons, and the children of daughters take the portions of daughters, however low in descent.

8. The second degree comprises the grandfather, and grandmother, and other ancestors, and brothers, and sisters, and their descendants, however low in descent, the nearer of whom exclude the more distant. The great-grandfather cannot inherit together with a grandfather or a grandmother; and the son of a brother cannot inherit with a brother or a sister, and the grandson of a brother cannot inherit with the son of a brother, or with the son of a sister.

9. This degree again is divided into two classes; the grand-parents and other ancestors, and the brethren and their descendants. Both these classes are unlimited, and their representatives in the ascending and descending line, may be extended *ad infinitum*. An individual of one class

does not exclude an individual of the other, though the relation to the deceased be more proximate; but the individuals of either class exclude each other in proportion to their proximity.

10. The third degree comprises the paternal and maternal uncles and aunts and their descendants, the nearer of whom exclude the more distant. The son of a paternal uncle cannot inherit with a paternal uncle, or a paternal aunt, nor the son of a maternal uncle with a maternal uncle or a maternal aunt.

11. This degree is unlimited in the ascending and descending line, and their representatives may be extended *ad infinitum;* but so long as there is a single aunt or uncle of the whole blood, the descendants of such persons cannot inherit. Uncles and aunts all share together; except some be of the half and others of the whole blood. A paternal uncle by the same father only is excluded by a paternal uncle by the same father and mother; and the son of a paternal uncle by the whole blood excludes a paternal uncle of the half blood.

12. In default of all the heirs above enumerated, the paternal and maternal uncles and aunts of the father and mother succeed, and in their default their descendants, to the remotest generation, according to their degree of proximity to the deceased. In default of all those heirs, the paternal and maternal uncles and aunts of the grandparents and great-grandparents inherit according to their degree of proximity to the deceased.*

* There seems to be some similarity between the order of succession here laid down, and that prescribed in the English Law for taking out letters of

13. It is a general rule that the individuals of the whole blood exclude those of the half blood who are of the same rank; but this rule does not apply to individuals of different ranks. For instance, a brother or sister of the whole blood excludes a brother or sister of the half blood: a son of the brother of the whole blood, however, does not exclude a brother of the half blood, because they belong to different ranks: but he would exclude a son of the half brother who is of the same rank; so also an uncle of the whole blood does not exclude a brother of the half blood, though he does an uncle of the half blood.

14. The principle of the whole blood excluding the half blood, is confined also to the same rank, among collaterals: for instance, generally a nephew or niece whose father was of the whole blood, does not exclude his or her uncle or aunt of the half blood; except in the case of there being a son of a paternal uncle of the whole blood, and a paternal uncle of the half blood by the same father only, the latter of whom is excluded by the former.

15. This principle of exclusion does not extend to uncles and aunts being of different sides of relation to the deceased; for instance, a paternal uncle or aunt of the whole blood does not exclude a maternal uncle

administration: "In the first place the children, or on failure of the children, the parents of the deceased, are entitled to the administration; both which indeed are in the first degree; but with us the children are allowed the preference. Then follow brothers, grandfathers, uncles or nephews (and the females of each class respectively), and lastly cousins. The half blood is admitted to the administration as well as the whole, for they are of the kindred of the Intestate." Blackstone's Com., vol. ii., p. 504.

or aunt of the half blood; but a paternal uncle or aunt of the whole blood excludes a paternal uncle or aunt of the half blood, and so likewise, a maternal uncle or aunt of the whole blood excludes a maternal uncle or aunt of the half blood.

16. If a man leave a paternal uncle of the half blood, and a maternal aunt of the whole blood, the former will take two-thirds in virtue of his claiming through the father, and the latter one-third in virtue of her claiming through the mother; as the property would have been divided between the parents in that proportion, had they been the claimants instead of the uncle and aunt.

17. The general rule, that those related by the same father and mother, exclude those who are related by the same mother only, does not operate in the case of individuals to whom a legal share has been assigned.

18. If a man leave a whole sister and a sister by the same mother only, the former will take half the estate and the latter one-sixth, the remainder reverting to the whole sister; and if there be more than one sister by the same mother only, they will take one-third and the remaining two-thirds will go to the whole sister.

19. Where there are two heirs, one of whom stands in a double relation: for instance, if a man die leaving a maternal uncle, and a paternal uncle who is also his maternal uncle,* the former will take one-third, and the

* The relation of paternal and maternal uncle may exist in the same person in the following manner: A having a son C by another wife, marries B having a daughter D by another husband. Then C and D intermarry and have issue, a son E, and A and B have a son F. Thus

latter two-thirds, and he will be further entitled to take one half of the third which devolved on the maternal uncle; and thus he will succeed altogether to five-sixths, leaving the other but one-sixth.

20. Secondly, those who succeed in virtue of marriage are the husband and wife, who can never be excluded in any possible case; and their shares are half for the husband, and a fourth for the wife, where there are no children, and a fourth for the husband, and an eighth for the wife, where there are children.

21. Where a wife dies, leaving no other heir, her whole property devolves on her husband; and where a husband dies leaving no other heir but his wife, she is only entitled to one-fourth of his property, and the remaining three-fourths will escheat to the public treasury.

22. If a sick man marry and die of that sickness without having consummated the marriage, his wife shall not inherit his estate; nor shall he inherit if his wife die before him, under such circumstances. But if a sick woman marry, and her husband die before her, she shall inherit of him, though the marriage was never consummated, and though she never recovered from that sickness.

23. If a man on his death bed divorce his wife, she shall inherit, provided he die of that sickness within one year from the period of divorce; but not if he lived for upwards of a year.

F is both the paternal and maternal uncle of E. So likewise if a person have a half brother by the same father, and a half sister by the same mother, who intermarry, he will necessarily be the paternal and maternal uncle of their issue.

24. In case of a reversible divorce, if the husband die within the period of his wife's probation, or if she die within that period, they have a mutual right to inherit each other's property.

25. The wife by an usufructuary, or temporary marriage, has no title to inherit.*

26. Thirdly, those who succeed in virtue of *Willa;* but they never can inherit so long as there is any claimant by consanguinity or marriage.

27. *Willa* is of two descriptions; that which is derived from manumission, where the emancipator by such act derives a right of inheritance; and that which depends on mutual compact, where two persons reciprocally engage, each to be heir of the other.

28. Claimants under the latter title are excluded by claimants under the former.

29. The general rules of exclusion, according to this sect, are similar to those contained in the orthodox doctrine; except that they make no distinction between male and female relations. Thus a daughter excludes a son's son, and a maternal uncle excludes a paternal grand uncle; whereas according to the orthodox doctrine in such cases, the daughter would get only half, and the maternal uncle would be wholly excluded by the paternal uncle of the father.

30. Difference of allegiance is no bar to inheritance, and homicide, whether justifiable or accidental, does not operate to exclude from the inheritance. The

* This species of contract is reprobated by the orthodox sect, and they are both considered wholly illegal. See Hamilton's Hedaya, vol. i., p. 71 and 72.

homicide, to disqualify, must have been of *malice prepense.*

31. The legal number of shares into which it is necessary to make the property, cannot be increased if found insufficient to satisfy all the heirs without a fraction. In such case a proportionate deduction will be made from the portion of such heir as may, under certain circumstances, be deprived of a legal share, or from any heir whose share admits of diminution. For instance, in the case of a husband, a daughter and parents. Here the property must be divided into twelve, of which the husband is entitled to three, or a fourth; the parents to two-sixths, or four, and the daughter to half; but there remain only five shares for her instead of six, or the moiety to which she is entitled. In this case, according to the orthodox doctrine, the property would have been made into thirteen parts to give the daughter her six shares; but according to the *Imamiya* tenets, the daughter must be content with the five shares that remain, because in certain cases her right as a legal sharer is liable to extinction; for instance, had there been a son, the daughter would not have been entitled to any specific share, and she would become a residuary; whereas the husband or parents can never be deprived of legal share, under any circumstances.

32. Where the assets exceed the number of heirs the surplus reverts to the heirs. The husband is entitled to share in the return; but not the wife. The mother also is not entitled to share in the return, if there are brethren: and where there is any individual possessing

a double relation, the surplus reverts exclusively to such individual.

33. On a distribution of the estate, the elder son, if he be worthy, is entitled to his father's sword, his Koran, his wearing apparel, and his ring.*

* In the foregoing summary I am not aware that I have omitted any point of material importance. The legal shares allotted to the several heirs are of course the same as those prescribed in the Súní Code, both having the precepts of the Koran as their guide. The rules of distribution and of ascertaining the relative shares of the different claimants are also (*mutatis mutandis*) the same. It is not worth while to notice in this compilation the doctrines of the *Imamiya* sect on the law of contracts, or their tenets in miscellaneous matters. A Digest of their laws, relative to those subjects, was some time ago prepared and a considerable part of it translated by an eminent Orientalist (Colonel John Baillie) by whom, however, it was left unfinished; probably from an opinion that the utility of the undertaking might not be commensurate to the time and labour employed upon it.

CHAPTER III.

OF SALE.

1. Sale is defined to be a mutual and voluntary exchange of property for property.

2. A contract of sale may be effected by the express agreement of the parties, or by reciprocal delivery.

3. Sale is of four kinds; consisting of commutation of goods for goods: of money for money: of money for goods: and of goods for money; which last is the most ordinary species of this kind of contract.

4. Sales are either absolute, conditional, or imperfect, or void.

5. An absolute sale is that which takes place immediately; there being no legal impediment.

6. A conditional sale is that which is suspended on the consent of the proprietor, or (where he is a minor) on the consent of his guardian, in which there is no legal impediment, and no condition requisite to its completion but such consent.

7. An imperfect sale is that which takes effect on seizin; the legal defect being cured by such seizin.

8. A void sale is that which can never take effect; in which the articles opposed to each other, or one of them, not bearing any legal value, the contract is null.

9. The consideration may consist of whatever articles, bearing a legal value, the seller and purchaser may agree upon; and the property may be sold for prime cost, or for more, or for less than prime cost.

10. It is requisite that there should be two parties to every contract of sale, except where the seller and purchaser employ the same agent, or where a father or a guardian makes a sale on behalf of a minor, or where a slave purchases his own freedom by permission of his master.

11. It is sufficient that the parties have a sense of the obligation they contract, and a minor, with the consent of his guardian, or a lunatic in his lucid intervals, may be contracting parties.

12. In a commutation of goods for goods, or of money for money, it is illegal to stipulate for a future period of delivery; but in a commutation of money for goods or of goods for money, such stipulation is authorised.

13. It is essential to the validity of every contract of sale, that the subject of it, and the consideration, should be so determinate as to admit of no future contention regarding the meaning of the contracting parties.

14. It is also essential that the subject of the contract should be in actual existence at the period of making the contract, or that it should be susceptible of delivery, either immediately or at some future definite period.

15. In a commutation of money for money or of goods for goods, if the articles opposed to each other are of the nature of similars, equality in point of quantity is an essential condition.

16. It is unlawful to stipulate for any extraneous condition, involving an advantage to either party, or for any uncertainty which might lead to future litigation; but if the extraneous condition be actually performed, or the uncertainty removed, the contract will stand good.

17. It is lawful to stipulate for an option of dissolving the contract; but the term stipulated should not exceed three days.

18. When payment is deferred to a future period, it must be determinate and cannot be suspended on an event, the time of the occurrence of which is uncertain, though its occurrence be inevitable. For instance, it is not lawful to suspend payment until the wind shall blow, or until it shall rain, nor is it lawful, even though the uncertainty be so inconsiderable as almost to amount to a fixed term; for instance, it is not lawful to suspend payment until the sowing or reaping time.

19. It is not lawful to sell property in exchange for a debt due from a third party, though it is for a debt due from the seller.

20. A resale of personal property cannot be made by the purchaser until the property shall actually have come into his possession.

21. A warranty as to freedom from defect and blemish, is implied in every contract of sale.

22. Where the property sold differs, either with

respect to quantity or quality from what the seller has described it, the purchaser is at liberty to recede from the contract.

23. By the sale of land, nothing thereon, which is of a transitory nature, passes. Thus the fruit of a tree belongs to the seller, though the tree itself, being a fixture, appertains to the purchaser of the land.

24. Where an option of dissolving the contract has been stipulated by the purchaser, and the property sold is injured or destroyed in his possession, he is responsible for the *price* agreed upon: but where the stipulation was on the part of the seller, the purchaser is responsible for the *value* only of the property.

25. But the condition of option is annulled by the purchaser's exercising any act of ownership, such as to take the property out of *statu quo*.

26. Where the property has not been seen by the purchaser, nor a sample (where a sample suffices), he is at liberty to recede from the contract, provided he may not have exercised any act of ownership; if upon seeing the property it does not suit his expectation, even though no option may have been stipulated.

27. But though the property have not been seen by the seller, he is not at liberty to recede from the contract (except in a sale of goods for goods), where no option was stipulated.

28. A purchaser who may not have agreed to take the property with all its faults, is at liberty to return it to the seller on the discovery of a defect, of which he was not aware at the time of the purchase, unless while in the

hands of the purchaser it received a further blemish; in which case he is only entitled to compensation.

29. But if the purchaser have sold such faulty article to a third person, he cannot exact compensation from the original seller; unless by having made an addition to the article prior to the sale, he was precluded from returning it to the original seller.

30. In a case where articles are sold, and are found on examination to be faulty, complete restitution of the price may be demanded from the seller, even though they have been destroyed in the act of trial, if the purchaser had not derived any benefit from them; but if the purchaser had made beneficial use of the faulty articles, he is only entitled to proportional compensation.

31. If a person sell an article which he had purchased, and be compelled to receive back such article and to refund the purchase money, he is entitled to the same remedy against the original seller, if the defect be of an inherent nature.

32. If a purchaser, after becoming aware of a defect in the article purchased, make use of the article or attempt to remove the defect, he shall have no remedy against the seller (unless there may have been some special clause in the contract); such act on his part implying acquiescence.

33. It is a general rule, that if the articles sold are of such a nature as not easily to admit of separation or division without injury, and part of them, subsequently to the purchase, be discovered to be defective, or to be the property of a third person, it is not competent to the

purchaser to keep a part and to return a part, demanding a proportional restitution of the price for the part returned. In this case he must either keep the whole, demanding compensation for the proportion that is defective, or he must return the whole, demanding complete restitution of the price. It is otherwise where the several parts may be separated without injury.

34. The practices of forestalling, regrating, and engrossing, and of selling on Friday, after the hour of prayer, are all prohibited, though they are valid.

CHAPTER IV.

OF SHUFAA, OR PRE-EMPTION.

1. *Shúfaa*, or the right of pre-emption, is defined to be a power of possessing property which has been sold, by paying a sum equal to that paid by the purchaser.

2. The right of pre-emption takes effect with regard to property sold, or parted with by some means equivalent to sale, but not with regard to property the possession of which has been transferred by gift, or by will, or by inheritance; unless the gift was made for a consideration, and the consideration was expressly stipulated; but pre-emption cannot be claimed where the donor has received a consideration for his gift, such consideration not having been expressly stipulated.

3. The right of pre-emption takes effect with regard to property whether divisible or indivisible; but it does not apply to moveable property, and it cannot take effect until after the sale is complete, as far as the interest of the seller is concerned.

4. The right of pre-emption may be claimed by all descriptions of persons. There is no distinction made on account of difference of religion.

5. All rights and privileges which belong to an ordinary purchaser, belong equally to a purchaser under the right of pre-emption.

6. The following persons may claim the right of pre-emption in the order enumerated: a partner in the property sold, a participator in its appendages, and a neighbour.

7. It is necessary that the person claiming this right, should declare his intention of becoming the purchaser, immediately on hearing of the sale, and that he should, with the least practicable delay, make affirmation, by witness, of such his intention, either in the presence of the seller, or of the purchaser, or on the premises.

8. The above preliminary conditions being fulfilled, the claimant of pre-emption is at liberty at any subsequent period to prefer his claim to a Court of Justice.*

9. The first purchaser has a right to retain the property until he has received the purchase money

* Much difference of opinion prevails as to this point. It seems equitable that there should be some limitation of time to bar a claim of this nature; otherwise a purchaser may be kept in a continual state of suspense. Ziffer and Mohammad are of opinion (and such also is the doctrine according to one tradition of Abú Yúsaf), that if the claimant causelessly neglect to advance his claim for a period exceeding one month, such delay shall amount to a defeasance of his right; but according to Abú Hanifa, and another tradition of Abú Yúsaf, there is no limitation as to time. This doctrine is maintained in the Fatáwa Aulamgírí, in the Mohitú Saruakhsí, and in the Hedaya; and it seems to be the most authentic and generally prevalent opinion. But the compiler of the Fatáwa Aulamgírí admits that decisions are given both ways.

from the claimant by pre-emption, and so also the seller in a case where delivery may not have been made.

10. Where an intermediate purchaser has made any improvements to the property, the claimant by pre-emption must either pay for their value, or cause them to be removed; and where the property may have been deteriorated by the act of the intermediate purchaser, he (the claimant) may insist on a proportional abatement of the price; but where the deterioration has taken place without the instrumentality of the intermediate purchaser, the claimant by pre-emption must either pay the whole price, or resign his claim altogether.

11. But a claimant by pre-emption having obtained possession of, and made improvements to property, is not entitled to compensation for such improvements, if it should afterwards appear that the property belonged to a third person. He will, in this case, recover the price from the seller or from the intermediate purchaser (if possession had been given), and he is at liberty to remove his improvements.

12. Where there is a dispute between the claimant by pre-emption and the purchaser, as to the price paid, and neither party have evidence, the assertion, on oath, of the purchaser must be credited; but where both parties have evidence, that of the claimant by pre-emption should be received in preference.

13. There are many legal devices by which the right of pre-emption may be defeated. For instance, where a man fears that his neighbour may advance such a claim,

he can sell all his property with the exception of that part immediately bordering on his neighbour's; and where he is apprehensive of the claim being advanced by a partner, he may, in the first instance, agree with the purchaser for some exorbitant nominal price, and afterwards commute that price for something of an inferior value; when, if a claimant by pre-emption appear, he must pay the price first stipulated, without reference to the subsequent commutation.

CHAPTER V.

OF GIFTS.

1. A gift is defined to be the conferring of property without a consideration.

2. Acceptance and seizin, on the part of the donee, are as necessary as relinquishment on the part of the donor.

3. A gift cannot be made to depend on a contingency, nor can it be referred to take effect at any future definite period.

4. It is necessary that a gift should be accompanied by delivery of possession, and that seizin should take effect immediately, or, if at a subsequent period, by desire of the donor.

5. A gift cannot be made of any thing to be produced *in futuro;* although the means of its production may be in the possession of the donee. The subject of the gift must be actually in existence at the time of the donation.

6. The gift of property which is undivided, and mixed with other property, admitting at the same time of division

or separation, is null and void, unless it be defined previous to delivery; for delivery of the gift cannot in that case be made without including something which forms no part of the gift.

7. In the case of a gift made to two or more donees, the interest of each donee must be defined either at the time of making the gift, or on delivery.

8. A gift cannot be implied. It must be express and unequivocal, and the intention of the donor must be demonstrated by his entire relinquishment of the thing given, and the gift is null and void where he continues to exercise any act of ownership over it.

9. The cases of a house given to a husband by a wife, and of property given by a father to his minor child, form exceptions to the above rule.

10. Formal delivery and seizin are not necessary in the case of a gift to a trustee, having the custody of the article given, nor in the case of a gift to a minor. The seizin of the guardian in the latter case is sufficient.

11. A gift on a deathbed is viewed in the light of a legacy, and cannot take effect for more than a third of the property; consequently no person can make a gift of any part of his property on his deathbed to one of his heirs, it not being lawful for one heir to take a legacy without the consent of the rest.

12. A donor is at liberty to resume his gift, except in the following instances:

13. A gift cannot be resumed where the donee is a relation; nor where anything has been received in return; nor where it has received any accession; nor where it has

come into possession of a second donee, or into that of the heirs of the first.

14. Besides the ordinary species of gift, the law enumerates two contracts under the head of gifts, which however more nearly resemble exchange or sale. They are technically termed *Hiba bil Iwaz*, mutual gift, or gift for a consideration, and *Hiba ba shart úl Iwaz*, gift on stipulation, or on promise of a consideration.

15. *Hiba bil Iwaz* is said to resemble a sale in all its properties; the same conditions attach to it, and the mutual seizin of the donees is not, in all cases, necessary.

16. *Hiba ba shart úl Iwaz*, on the other hand, is said to resemble a sale in the first stage only; that is, before the consideration for which the gift is made has been received, and the seizin of the donor and donee is therefore a requisite condition.

CHAPTER VI.

OF WILLS.

1. There is no preference shown to a written over a nuncupative will, and they are entitled to equal weight, whether the property which is the subject of the will be real or personal.

2. Legacies cannot be made to a larger amount than one-third of the testator's estate without the consent of the heirs.

3. A legacy cannot be left to one of the heirs without the consent of the rest.

4. There is this difference between the property which is the subject of inheritance and that which is the subject of legacy. The former becomes the property of the heir by the mere operation of law; the other does not become the property of the legatee until his consent shall have been obtained either expressly or impliedly.

5. The payment of legacies to a legal amount precedes the satisfaction of claims of inheritance.

6. All the debts due by the testator must be liquidated before the legacies can be claimed.

7. An acknowledgment of debt in favour of an heir on a deathbed resembles a legacy; inasmuch as it does not avail for more than a third of the estate.

8. It is not necessary that the subject of the legacy should exist at the time of the execution of the will. It is sufficient for its validity that it should be in existence at the time of the death of the testator.

9. The general validity of a will is not affected by its containing illegal provisions, but it will be carried into execution as far as it may be consistent with law.

10. A person not being an heir at the time of the execution of the will, but becoming one previous to the death of the testator, cannot take the legacy left to him by such will; but a person being an heir at the time of the execution, and becoming excluded previously to the testator's death, can take the legacy left to him by such will.

11. If a man bequeath property to one person, and subsequently make a bequest of the same property to another individual, the first bequest is annulled; so also if he sell or give the legacy to any other individual; even though it may have reverted to his possession before his death, as these acts amount to a retractation of the legacy.

12. Where a testator bequeaths more than he legally can to several legatees, and the heirs refuse to confirm his disposition, a proportionate abatement must be made in all the legacies.

13. Where a legacy is left to an individual, and subsequently a larger legacy to the same individual, the

larger legacy will take effect; but where the larger legacy was prior to the smaller one, the latter only will take effect.

14. A legacy being left to two persons indiscriminately, if one of them die before the legacy is payable, the whole will go to the survivor; but if half was left to each of them, the survivor will get only half, and the remaining moiety will devolve on the heirs; so also in the case of an heir and stranger being left joint legatees.

15. Where there is no executor appointed, the father or the grandfather may act as executor, or in their default their executors.

16. A Mohammadan should not appoint a person of a different persuasion to be his executor, and such appointment is liable to be annulled by the ruling power.

17. Executors having once accepted cannot subsequently decline the trust.

18. Where there are two executors, it is not competent to one of them to act singly, except in cases of necessity, and where benefit to the estate must certainly accrue.

CHAPTER VII.

OF MARRIAGE, DOWER, DIVORCE, AND PARENTAGE.

1. Marriage is defined to be a contract founded on the intention of legalizing generation.

2. Proposal and consent are essential to a contract of marriage.

3. The conditions are discretion, puberty, and freedom of the contracting parties. In the absence of the first condition, the contract is void *ab initio;* for a marriage cannot be contracted by an infant without discretion, nor by a lunatic. In the absence of the two latter conditions the contract is voidable; for the validity of marriages contracted by discreet minors, or slaves, is suspensive on the consent of their guardians or masters. It is also necessary that there should be no legal incapacity on the part of the woman; that each party should know the agreement of the other; that there should be witnesses to the contract, and that the proposal and acceptance should be made at the same time and place.

4. There are only four requisites to the competency of witnesses to a marriage contract; namely, freedom, discretion, puberty, and profession of the Músalmán faith.

5. Objections as to character and relation do not apply to witnesses in a contract of marriage as they do in other contracts.

6. A proposal may be made by means of agency, or by letter; provided there are witnesses to the receipt of the message or letter, and to the consent on the part of the person to whom it was addressed.

7. The effect of a contract of marriage is to legalize the mutual enjoyment of the parties; to place the wife under the dominion of the husband; to confer on her the right of dower, maintenance,* and habitation; to create between the parties, prohibited degrees of relation and reciprocal right of inheritance; to enforce equality of behaviour towards all his wives on the part of the husband, and obedience on the part of the wife, and to invest the husband with a power of correction in cases of disobedience.

8. A freeman may have four wives, but a slave can have only two.

9. A man may not marry his mother, nor his grandmother, nor his mother-in-law, nor his step-mother, nor his step-grandmother, nor his daughter, nor his grand-daughter, nor his daughter-in-law, nor his grand-daughter-

* The right of a wife to maintenance is expressly recognized: so much so, that if the husband be absent and have not made any provision for his wife, the Law will cause it to be made out of his property; and in case of divorce, the wife is entitled to maintenance during the period of her probation.

in-law, nor his step-daughter, nor his sister, nor his foster-sister, nor his niece, nor his aunt, nor his nurse.

10. Nor is it lawful for a man to be married at the same time to any two women who stand in such a degree of relation to each other, as that, if one of them had been a male, they could not have intermarried.

11. Marriage cannot be contracted with a person who is a slave of the party; but the union of a freeman with a slave, not being his property, with the consent of the master of such slave, is admissible, provided he be not already married to a freewoman.

12. Christians, Jews, and persons of other religions, believing in one God, may be espoused by Mohammadans.

13. Marriage will be presumed, in a case of proved continual cohabitation, without the testimony of witnesses; but the presence of witnesses is nevertheless requisite at all nuptials.

14. A woman having attained the age of puberty, may contract herself in marriage with whomsoever she pleases; and her guardian has no right to interfere if the match be equal.

15. If the match be unequal, the guardians have a right to interfere with a view to set it aside.

16. A female not having attained the age of puberty, cannot lawfully contract herself in marriage without the consent of her guardians, and the validity of the contract entirely depends upon such consent.

17. But in both the preceding cases the guardians should interfere before the birth of issue.

18. A contract of marriage entered into by a father or grandfather, on behalf of an infant, is valid and binding, and the infant has not the option of annulling it on attaining maturity; but if entered into by any other guardian, the infant so contracted may dissolve the marriage on coming of age, provided that such delay does not take place as may be construed into acquiescence.

19. Where there is no paternal guardian, the maternal kindred may dispose of an infant in marriage; and in default of maternal guardians the government may supply their place.

20. A necessary concomitant of a contract of marriage is dower, the maximum of which is not fixed, but the minimum is ten dirms,* and it becomes due on the consummation of the marriage (though it is usual to stipulate for delay as to the payment of a part) or on the death of either party or on divorce.

21. Where no amount of dower has been specified, the woman is entitled to receive a sum equal to the average rate of dower granted to the females of her father's family.

22. Where it may not have been expressed whether the payment of the dower is to be prompt or deferred, it must be held that the whole is due on demand.

23. It is a rule that whatsoever is prohibited by reason of consanguinity is prohibited by reason of

* The value of the dirm is very uncertain. Ten dirms according to one account make about six shillings and eight pence sterling. See note to Hamilton's translation of the Hedaya, p. 122, vol. i.

fosterage; but as far as marriage is concerned, there are one or two exceptions to this rule: for instance, a man may marry his sister's foster-mother, or his foster-sister's mother, or his foster-son's sister, or his foster-brother's sister.

24. A husband may divorce his wife without any misbehaviour on her part, or without assigning any cause; but before the divorce becomes irreversible, according to the more approved doctrine, it must be repeated three times, and between each time the period of one month must have intervened, and in the interval he may take her back either in an express or implied manner.

25. A husband cannot again cohabit with his wife who has been three times irreversibly divorced, until after she shall have been married to some other individual and separated from him either by death or divorce; but this is not necessary to a reunion, if she have been separated by only one or two divorces.

26. If a husband divorce his wife on his death-bed, she is nevertheless entitled to inherit, if he die before the expiration of the term (four months and ten days) of probation, which she is bound to undergo before contracting a second marriage.

27. A vow of abstinence made by a husband, and maintained inviolate for a period of four months, amounts to an irreversible divorce.*

* There is recognized a species of reversible divorce, which is effected by the husband comparing his wife to any member of his mother, or some other relation prohibited to him, which must be expiated by emancipating a slave, by alms or by fasting. This divorce is technically termed *Zihar.* Hedaya, book iv., chap. ix.

28. A wife is at liberty, with her husband's consent, to purchase from him her freedom from the bonds of marriage.

29. Another mode of separation is by the husband's making oath, accompanied by an imprecation as to his wife's fidelity, and if he in the same manner deny the parentage of the child of which she is then pregnant, it will be bastardized.

30. Established impotency is also a ground for admitting a claim to separation on the part of the wife.

31. A child born six months after marriage is considered to all intents and purposes the offspring of the husband; so also a child born within two years after the death of her husband or after divorce.

32. The first born child of a man's female slave is considered his offspring, provided he claim the parentage, but not otherwise: but if after his having claimed the parentage of one, the same woman bear another child to him, the parentage of that other will be established without any claim on his part.

33. If a man acknowledge another to be his son, and there be nothing which obviously renders it impossible that such relation should exist between them, the parentage will be established.

CHAPTER VIII.

OF GUARDIANS AND MINORITY.

1. All persons, whether male or female, are considered minors until after the expiration of the sixteenth year, unless symptoms of puberty appear at an earlier period.

2. There is a subdivision of the state of minority, though not so minute as in the Civil Law, the term minor being used indiscriminately to signify all persons under the age of puberty; but the term *Saḅi* is applied to persons in a state of infancy, and the term *Múrahik* to those who have nearly attained puberty.*

* "The great distinction was therefore into majors and minors; but minors were again subdivided into *Puberes* and *Impuberes*; and *Impuberes* again underwent a subdivision into *Infantes* and *Impuberes*." Summary of Taylor's Roman Law, p. 124. In the Mohammadan Law a person after attaining majority is termed *Shab* till the age of thirty-four years; he is termed *Kohal* until the age of fifty-one, and *Sheikh* for the remainder of his life.

3. Minors have not different privileges at different stages of their minority, as in the English law.*

4. Guardians are either natural or testamentary.

5. They are also near and remote. Of the former description are fathers and paternal grandfathers and their executors and the executors of such executors. Of the latter description are the more distant paternal kindred, and their guardianship extends only to matters connected with the education and marriage of their wards.

6. The former description of guardians answers to the term of curator in the Civil Law, and of manager in the Bengal Code of Regulations; having power over the property of a minor for purposes beneficial to him; and in their default this power does not vest in the remote guardians, but devolves on the ruling authority.

7. Maternal relations are the lowest species of guardians, as their right of guardianship for the purposes of education and marriage takes effect only where there may be no paternal kindred nor mother.

8. Mothers have the right (and widows *durante*

* The ages of male and female are different for different purposes. A male at twelve years old may take the oath of allegiance; at fourteen is at years of discretion, and therefore may consent or disagree to marriage, may choose his guardian, and, if his discretion be actually proved, may make his testament of his personal estate; at seventeen may be an executor, and at twenty-one is at his own disposal, and may alienate his lands, goods, and chattels. A female also at seven years of age may be betrothed or given in marriage; at nine is entitled to a dower; at twelve is at years of maturity, and therefore may consent or disagree to marriage, and if proved to have sufficient discretion, may bequeath her personal estate; at fourteen is at years of legal discretion, and may choose a guardian; at seventeen may be executress; and at twenty-one may dispose of herself and her lands.—See Blackstone's Com., vol. i., p. 463.

viduitate) to the custody of their sons until they attain the age of seven years, and of their daughters until they attain the age of puberty.

9. The mother's right is forfeited by marrying a stranger, but reverts on her again becoming a widow.

10. The paternal relations succeed to the right of guardianship, for the purposes of education and marriage, in proportion to the proximity of their claims to inherit the estate of the minor.

11. Necessary debts contracted by any guardian for the support or education of his ward must be discharged by him on his coming of age.

12. A minor is not competent *sui juris* to contract marriage, to pass a divorce, to manumit a slave, to make a loan, or contract a debt, or to engage in any other transaction of a nature not manifestly for his benefit, without the consent of his guardian.

13. But he may receive a gift, or do any other act which is manifestly for his benefit.

14. A guardian is not at liberty to sell the immoveable property of his ward, except under seven circumstances, viz. 1st, where he can obtain double its value; 2ndly, where the minor has no other property, and the sale of it is absolutely necessary to his maintenance; 3rdly, where the late incumbent died in debt which cannot be liquidated but by the sale of such property; 4thly, where there are some general provisions in the will which cannot be carried into effect without such sale; 5thly, where the produce of the property is not sufficient to defray the expences of keeping it; 6thly, where the property may be

in danger of being destroyed; 7thly, where it has been usurped, and the guardian has reason to fear that there is no chance of fair restitution.

15. Every contract entered into by a near guardian on behalf and for the benefit of the minor, and every contract entered into by a minor with the advice and consent of his near guardian, as far as regards his personal property, is valid and binding upon him; provided there be no circumvention or fraud on the face of it.

16. Minors are civilly responsible for any intentional damage or injury done by them to the property or interests of others, though they are not liable in criminal matters to retaliation or to the *ultimum supplicium*, but they are liable to discretionary chastisement and correction.

CHAPTER IX.

OF SLAVERY.

1. There are only two descriptions of persons recognized as slaves under the Mohammadan Law. First, infidels made captive during war; and secondly, their descendants. These persons are subjects of inheritance, and of all kinds of contracts, in the same manner as other property.

2. The general state of bondage is subdivided into two classes, and slavery may be either entire or qualified, according to circumstances.

3. Qualified slaves are of three descriptions: the *Múkátib*; the *Múdabbir*, and the *Um-i-walad.*

4. A *Múkátib* slave is he between whom and his master there may have been an agreement for his ransom, on the condition of his paying a certain sum of money, either immediately, or at some future time, or by instalments.

5. If he fulfil the condition he will become free; otherwise he will revert to his former unqualified state of bondage. In the mean time his master parts with

the possession of, but not with the property in him. He is not, however, in the interval a fit subject of sale, gift, pledge or hire.

6. A *Múdabbir* slave is he to whom his master has promised *post-obit* emancipation; such promise however may be made absolutely, or with limitation; in other words the freedom of the slave may be made to depend generally on the death of his master, whenever that event may happen: or it may be made conditionally, to depend on the occurrence of the event within a specified period.

7. This description of slave is not a fit subject of sale or gift, but labour may be exacted from him and he may be let out to hire, and in the case of a female she may be given in marriage. Where the promise was made absolutely, the slave becomes free on the death of the master, whenever that event may happen; and, where made conditionally, if his death occurred within the period specified.

8. The general law of legacies and debts is applicable to this description of slaves, they being considered as much the right of heirs as any other description of property: consequently they can only be emancipated to the extent of one-third of the value of their persons, where the master leaves no other property; and they must perform emancipatory labour for the benefit of the heirs to the extent of the other two-thirds; and where the master dies insolvent, they do not become free until, for the benefit of the deceased's creditors, they have earned by their labour property to the full amount of their value.

9. An *Um-i-walad* is a female slave who has borne a child or children to her master.

10. The law is the same regarding this description of slave as regarding the *Múdabbir*, with this difference in her favour, that she is emancipated unconditionally on the death of her master; whether he may or may not have left other assets, or whether he may have died in a state of insolvency or otherwise. But it should be observed that the parentage of such slave is not established in her master unless he acknowledge the first born.

11. Slaves labour under almost every species of incapacity. They cannot marry without the consent of their masters. Their evidence is not admissible, nor their acknowledgments (unless they are licensed) in matters relative to property. They are not generally eligible to fill any civil office in the state, nor can they be executors, sureties or guardians (unless to the minor children of their masters by special appointment) nor are they competent to make a gift or sale, nor to inherit or bequeath property.

12. But, as some counterpoise to these disqualifications, they are exempted from many obligations of freedom. They are not liable to be sued except in the presence of their masters; they are not subject to the payment of taxes, and they cannot be imprisoned for debt. In criminal matters the indulgences extended to them are more numerous.

13. Any description of slave however may be licensed, either for a particular purpose or generally for commercial transactions; in which case they are allowed to act to the extent of their license.

14. Masters may compel their slaves to marry. Un-

qualified slaves may be sold to make good their wives' dower and maintenance, and qualified slaves may be compelled to labour for the same purposes. A man cannot marry a female slave so long as he has a free wife; nor can he under any circumstances marry his own slave girl, nor can a slave marry his mistress.

15. Persons who stand reciprocally related within the prohibited degrees cannot be the slaves of each other.

16. Where issue has been begotten between the male slave of one person and the female slave of another, the maxim of *partus sequitur ventrem* applies, and the former has no legal claim to the children so begotten.

17. It is a question how far the sale of a man's own person is lawful when reduced to extreme necessity. It is declared justifiable in the *Mohít-ú-sarakhsi*, a work of unexceptionable authority. But while deference is paid to that authority, by admitting the validity of the sale, it is nevertheless universally contended that it should be cancelled on the application of the slave, and that he should be compelled by his labour to refund the value of what he had received from his purchaser.

18. It is admitted however by all authorities that a person may hire himself for any time, even though it amount to servitude for life; but minors so hired may annul the contract on attaining majority.

CHAPTER X.

OF ENDOWMENTS.

1. An endowment signifies the appropriation of property to the service of God; when the right of the appropriator becomes divested, and the profits of the property so appropriated are devoted to the benefit of mankind.

2. An endowment is not a fit subject of sale, gift, or inheritance; and if the appropriation is made *in extremis*, it takes effect only to the extent of a third of the property of the appropriator. Undefined property is a fit subject of endowment.

3. Endowed property may be sold by judicial authority, when the sale may be absolutely necessary to defray the expense of repairing its edifices or other indispensible purposes, and where the object cannot be attained by farming or other temporary expedient.

4. In case of the grant of an endowment to an individual with reversion to the poor, it is not necessary that the grantees specified shall be in existence at the time. For instance, if the grant be made in the name of the children of A with reversion to the poor, and A should prove to have no children, the grant would nevertheless be valid, and the profits of the endowment will be distributed among the poor.

5. The ruling power cannot remove the superintendent of an endowment appointed by the appropriator, unless on proof of misconduct; nor can the appropriator himself remove such person, unless the liberty of doing so may have been specially reserved to him at the time of his making the appropriation.

6. Where the appropriator of an endowment may not have made any express provision as to who shall succeed to the office of superintendent on the death of the person nominated by himself, and he may not have left an executor, such superintendent may, on his deathbed, appoint his own successor, subject to the confirmation of the ruling power.

7. The specific property endowed cannot be exchanged for other property, unless a stipulation to this effect may have been made by the appropriator, or unless circumstances should render it impracticable to retain possession of the particular property, or unless manifest advantage be derivable from the exchange; nor should endowed lands be farmed out on terms inferior to their value, nor for a longer period than three years, except when circumstances render such measure absolutely necessary to the preservation of the endowment.

8. The injunctions of the appropriator should be observed except in the following cases: If he stipulate that the superintendent shall not be removed by the ruling authorities, such person is nevertheless removeable by them on proof of misconduct. If he stipulate that the appropriated lands shall not be let out to farm for a longer period than one year, and it be difficult to obtain a tenant

for so short a period or, by making a longer lease, it be better calculated to promote the interests of the establishment, the ruling authorities are at liberty to act without the consent of the superintendent. If he stipulate that the excess of the profits be distributed among persons who beg for it in the mosque, it may nevertheless be distributed in other places and among the necessitous, though not beggars. If he stipulate that daily rations of food be served out to the necessitous, the allowance may nevertheless be made in money. The ruling authorities have power to increase the salaries of the officers attached to the endowment, when they appear deserving of it, and the endowed property may be exchanged, when it may seem advantageous, by order of such authorities; even though the appropriator may have expressly stipulated against an exchange.

9. Where an appropriator appoints two persons joint superintendents, it is not competent to either of them to act separately; but where he himself retains a moiety of the superintendence, associating another individual, he (the appropriator) is at liberty to act singly and of his own authority in his self-created capacity of joint superintendent.

10. Where an appropriation has been made by the ruling power, from the funds of the public treasury, for public purposes, without any specific nomination, the superintendence should be entrusted to some person most deserving in point of learning; but in private appropriations, with the exceptions above mentioned, the injunctions of the founder should be fulfilled.

CHAPTER XI.

OF DEBTS AND SECURITIES.

1. Heirs are answerable for the debts of their ancestors, as far as there are assets.

2. The payment of debts acknowledged on a deathbed must be postponed until after the liquidation of those contracted in health, unless it be notorious that the former were *bonâ fide* contracted; and a deathbed acknowledgement of a debt in favour of an heir is entirely null and void, unless the other heirs admit that it is due.

3. If two persons jointly contract a debt and one of them die, the survivor will be held responsible for a moiety only of the debt; unless there was an express stipulation that each should be liable for the whole amount: for the law presumes that each were equal participators in the profits of the loan, and that one should not be responsible for the share of advantage acquired by the other.

4. So also where two persons are joint sureties for the payment of a debt, if one of them die, the survivor will

not be considered as surety for the whole, and that the one should be surety for the other.

5. It is different where two partners are engaged in traffic, contributing the same amount in capital, and being equal in all respects, in which case the one partner is responsible for all acts done and for all debts contracted by the other. But this is not the case with regard to other partnerships, in which case a creditor of the concern cannot claim the whole debt from any one of the partners severally, but must either come upon the whole collectively, or if he prefer his claim against any one individual partner, it must be only to the extent of his share.

6. Necessary debts contracted by a guardian on account of his ward must be discharged by the latter on his coming of age.

7. A general inhibition cannot be laid on a debtor to exclude him entirely from the management of his own affairs; but he may be restrained from entering into such contracts as are manifestly injurious to his creditor.

8. If a debtor, on being sued, acknowledge the debt, he must not be immediately imprisoned, but if he deny, and it be established by evidence, he should be committed forthwith to jail.

9. If, after judgment, there should be any procrastination on the part of a debtor who has been suffered to go at large, and he may have received a valuable consideration for the debt, or if it be a debt on beneficial contract, he should be committed to jail notwithstanding he plead poverty.

10. But if the debt had been contracted gratuitously

and without any valuable consideration having been received (as in the case of a debt contracted by a surety on account of his principal), the debtor should not be imprisoned unless the creditor can establish his solvency.

11. It is left discretionary with the judicial authorities to determine the period of imprisonment in cases of apparent insolvency.

12. But the liberation of a debtor does not exempt him from all future pursuit by his creditors. They may cause his arrest at a subsequent period, on proof of his ability to discharge the debt.

13. In the attachment and sale of property belonging to a debtor, great caution is prescribed. In the first place, his money should be applied to the liquidation of his debt; next, his personal effects, and last of all his houses and lands.

14. There is no distinction between mortgages of lands and pledges of goods.

15. Hypothecation is unknown to the Mohammadan Law, and seizin is a requisite condition of mortgage.

16. The creditor is not at liberty to alienate and sell the mortgage or pledge at any time, unless there was an express agreement to that effect between him and the debtor, as the property mortgaged is presumed to be equivalent to the debt, and as the debt cannot receive any accession, interest being prohibited.

17. It is a general rule that the pawnee is chargeable with the expence of providing for the custody, and the pawner with the expence of providing for the support of the thing pledged; for instance, in the case of a pledge of

a horse, it is necessary that the pawner should provide his food, and the pawnee his stable.

18. Where property may have been pawned or mortgaged in satisfaction of a debt, it is not lawful for the pawnee or mortgagee to use it without the consent of the pawner or mortgager, and if he do so, he is responsible for the whole value.

19. Where such property, being equivalent to the debt, may have been destroyed otherwise than by the act of the pawnee or mortgagee, the debt is extinguished; where it exceeds the debt, the pawnee or mortgagee is not responsible for the excess, but where it falls short of the debt, the deficiency must be made up by the pawner or mortgager; but if the property were wilfully destroyed by the act of the pawnee or mortgagee, he will be responsible for any excess of its value beyond the amount of the debt.

20. If a person die, leaving many creditors, and he may have pawned or mortgaged some property to one of them, such creditor is at liberty to satisfy his own debt out of the property of the deceased debtor, which is in his own possession, to the exclusion of all the other creditors.

CHAPTER XII.

OF CLAIMS AND JUDICIAL MATTERS.

1. There is no rule of limitation to bar a claim of right according to the Mohammadan Law.*

2. A claim founded on a verbal engagement is of equal weight with a claim founded on a written engagement.

3. Informality in a deed does not vitiate a contract founded thereon, provided the intention of the contracting parties can otherwise be clearly ascertained.

4. The general rule with respect to all claims is that priority in point of time confers superiority of right.

5. Where the priority of either cannot be ascertained, a claim founded on purchase is entitled to the preference over a claim founded on gift.

* In the *Bahr-ú-rayik* an opinion is cited from the Mabsút, to the effect that if a person causelessly neglect to advance his claim for a period of thirty-three years, it shall not be cognizable in a court of justice; but this opinion is adverse to the received legal doctrine.

6. Contracts are not dissolved generally by the death of one of the contracting parties, but they devolve on the representatives as far as there are assets; unless the subject of the contract be of a personal nature, such for instance, as in the case of a lease, if either the landlord or the farmer die, the contract ceases on the occurrence of that event.

7. So also in the case of partnership and joint concerns of any description, where the surviving partners are not bound to continue in business with the heirs of the deceased partner, and *vice versa*; and the obligation is extinguished, as well by civil as by natural death.

8. Oaths are not administered to witnesses.

9. In civil claims the evidence of two men, or one man and two women is generally requisite.

10. Slaves, minors and persons convicted of slander are not competent witnesses.

11. The evidence of a father or grandfather, in favour of his son or his grandson, and *vice versa;* of a husband in favour of his wife, and *vice versa,* and of a servant in favour of his master, and *vice versa,* is not admissible.

12. Nor is the evidence of a partner admissible in matters affecting the joint concern.

13. In matters which fall peculiarly within the province of women, female evidence is admissible, uncorroborated by male testimony.

14. Hearsay evidence is admissible to establish birth, death, marriage, cohabitation, and the appointment of a Kazí; as the eye-witnesses to such transactions are frequently not forthcoming.

15. No respect is paid to any superiority in the number of witnesses above the prescribed number adduced in support of a claim.

16. The evidence of witnesses which tends to establish the plaintiff's claim to any thing not contained in his own statement, must be rejected; for instance, if any of his witnesses depose to a larger sum being due to him than that claimed by himself.

17. The evidence of witnesses which tends to establish the plaintiff's claim on a ground different from that alleged by himself, must be rejected; for instance, if the plaintiff were to claim by purchase and his witnesses were to depose to his claim being founded on gift.

18. Where a debt is claimed, and some of the witnesses depose to the debt of the whole sum claimed and others to a part of it only, the plaintiff is entitled to such part only of the sum claimed.

19. Where a defendant pleads the general issue, the *onus probandi* rests on the plaintiff.

20. Where a plea contains defensive matter, such as payment or satisfaction, the *onus probandi* rests on the defendant; the rule being the same as in the Civil Law, that in every issue the affirmative is to be proved.

21. A defendant may in some cases plead both the general issue and a special plea, where they are not inconsistent; and the *onus probandi* in such case rests on the plaintiff, where the special plea is not necessary to the defence; for instance, a man sues another for half an estate, alleging that he was born in wedlock of the same

father and mother as the defendant. Here the defendant may deny the allegation generally and at the same time plead that the defendant was born of a different family.

22. A claim is not admissible which may be repugnant to a former claim, both of which cannot stand; for instance, a person in a former suit having denied that a certain individual was his brother, cannot subsequently claim the inheritance of that person on the plea of such relation.

23. But if the claim be at variance with a former one, and they can both consistently stand, it is admissible; for instance, a claim having been advanced to property in virtue of purchase, the same property may be claimed by the same person in virtue of inheritance, but if the claim of inheritance had been prior, a subsequent claim of purchase is not admissible; as it is manifest that they cannot both consistently stand.*

24. If a man adduce a claim and have no evidence to support it, the general rule is, that the defendant must be put to his oath, and if he decline swearing, judgment should be given for the plaintiff; but if he deny on oath, he is absolved from the claim.

25. Where both parties have evidence, that of the plaintiff is generally entitled to preference. Thus, for

* At first sight there might appear to be a distinction without a difference in this case; but the reason of the rule is that an heir might consistently make a purchase of property which had not devolved, but of which he was in expectancy. But it is contrary to all probability that he should have purchased, after the demise of the ancestor, property to which he had represented himself actually entitled in virtue of inheritance.

instance, where the creditor and debtor are at issue as to the amount of a debt, and both parties have evidence, that of the former is entitled to preference; but where neither party has evidence, the assertion on oath of the latter is to be credited.

26. It is also a general principle that where there is evidence adduced on both sides, *ceteris paribus*, the preference should be given to the witnesses of the party whose claim is greater, or who has the greater interest in the subject matter. Thus, for instance, in an action arising out of a contract of sale, where there is a disagreement about the price between the seller and purchaser, both parties having evidence, the witnesses who depose to the larger sum being due, that is of the plaintiff, are entitled to preference.

27. And where there is a disagreement, both as to the price and goods, both parties having witnesses, the evidence adduced by the seller is entitled to preference as far as it affects the amount of price, and that of the purchaser as far as it affects the quality and quantity of the goods.

28. If neither party have evidence, they should both be put to their oaths, and if both consent to swear, the contract must be dissolved; but if one decline and the other swear the decree should be passed in favour of the swearer.

29. But if the disagreement exist with respect to the conditions only of a sale, such as the period of payment, etc., and both parties consent to swear, the assertion on oath of the party against whom the claim is made is entitled to preference.

30. Where a husband and wife dispute as to the amount of dower, both parties having evidence, that of the wife must be credited as it proves most;* so also in a dispute between a lessor and lessee, the evidence of each party is entitled to preference as far as their individual interests are at stake; the evidence of the lessor being received as to the amount of the rent, and that of the lessee as to the duration of the term.

31. Where property is claimed and the person in whose possession it is, states that he is merely a depositary or a pawnee of an absent proprietor, and adduces evidence in support of his assertion, the claim must be dismissed; but the claim should be rejected *in limine* where the claimant admits his title to have been derived from such absentee proprietor.

32. Judgment cannot be passed *ex parte*, the reason given being, that decisions must be founded either on the defendant's confession, or (notwithstanding his denial) on proof by witnesses; and where he is absent, it cannot be said whether he would have denied or admitted the claim.

33. When cases are referred to arbitration, it is requisite that the decision of the arbitrators should be unanimous.

* But there is an exception to this general rule. If the proper dower of the wife, that is to say the average rate of dower paid to her paternal female relations, exceed the amount claimed by her, the evidence adduced by the husband is entitled to preference, because that goes to prove some remission on her part. See Hedaya, vol. i., p. 154.